TAROT MAGIC

ABOUT THE AUTHOR

Donald Tyson has been writing about the Tarot and other New Age and esoteric subjects for more than fifteen years and is the author of over a dozen books. He lives in Nova Scotia, Canada.

TAROT MAGIC

Ceremonial Magic Using
Golden Dawn Correspondences

DONALD TYSON

Llewellyn Publications
Woodbury, Minnesota

First Edition
Second Printing, 2018

Book design and layout by Joanna Willis
Cover design by Shira Atakpu
Interior illustrations by Llewellyn art department

Previously published as *Portable Magic*
Llewellyn is a registered trademark of Llewellyn Worldwide Ltd.

Library of Congress Cataloging-in-Publication Data
Tyson, Donald, 1954–
    Portable magic : tarot is the only tool you need / Donald Tyson.—1st ed.
        p. cm.
    Includes bibliographical references and index.
    ISBN-13: 978-0-7387-0980-2
    ISBN-10: 0-7387-0980-8
    1. Tarot. 2. Magic. 3. Ritual. I. Title.

BF1879.T2T98 2006
133.3'2424—dc22

                                                                2006047276

Llewellyn Publications
A Division of Llewellyn Worldwide Ltd.
2143 Wooddale Drive
Woodbury, MN 55125-2989
www.llewellyn.com

Printed in the United States of America

ALSO BY DONALD TYSON

1-2-3 Tarot

Alhazred

Enochian Magic for Beginners

Familiar Spirits

Necronomicon

The Power of the Word

Ritual Magic

Scrying for Beginners

Three Books of Occult Philosophy

The 13 Gates of the Necronomicon

The Fourth Book of Occult Philosophy

The Demonology of King James I

Grimoire of the Necronomicon

Necronomicon Tarot (with Anne Stokes)

Runic Astrology

Serpent of Wisdom

Soul Flight

The Dreamworld of H. P. Lovecraft

CONTENTS

1

WHAT IS
TAROT MAGIC?

When you think of the Tarot, you probably think of fortune telling. This is not surprising since divination has been the main function of Tarot cards for more than two hundred years. Only in the late eighteenth century did the symbolism on the cards acquire a higher spiritual meaning and come to be regarded as an important part of the Western esoteric tradition. In spite of its elevation from the mundane to the mysterious, the primary use for the Tarot remains fortune telling even in the present day. If you examine the books available on the Tarot, most are about divination, with only a handful devoted to the higher meaning of Tarot symbolism.

There is another side to the Tarot that is little known and less understood. The cards can be used as potent instruments of ritual magic. This active function of the Tarot has always existed, but is overlooked or ignored even by many of the greatest modern ceremonial magicians, who regard the Tarot either as an instrument of fortune telling or as a source of symbolism suitable for meditation. It is much more, as this book will show.

A deck of Tarot cards contains everything you need to work a complete and effective system of ritual magic. With the cards alone, you can construct an astral temple, build an altar, cast a magic circle, create a triangle through which to actualize your purpose, manipulate the blind elemental forces of nature, communicate with other people and with spirits, cleanse atmospheres and places of destructive influences, make potent charms, extend aid, and perform works of healing. You can attract wealth, gain love, or achieve victory over your enemies. You can use the Tarot to accomplish any purpose you would seek to achieve through more cumbersome and complex methods of ceremonial magic.

All this with only a deck of Tarot cards. When your work is done, you simply fold the cards together and put your temple, your altar, your circle, your triangle, and all your instruments into your pocket, ready for the next time you need them. Tarot magic requires no expensive materials or hand-crafted tools, no incense, no candles, no oils, no arcane languages, no special place in which to work, no costly robes or talismans. Yet it is as effective as the most complex system of magic. Everything is done through the symbolism of the cards, in accord with the esoteric correspondences for the Tarot set forth by the Hermetic Order of the Golden Dawn.

The standard Golden Dawn correspondences for the Tarot are used throughout this book because they are the most widely understood and accepted. Those familiar with my other writings know that I have made modifications to these correspondences in my personal esoteric system, but in this general text on Tarot magic I prefer to retain the correspondences with which most readers will be familiar in order to minimize confusion. It is a simple matter to adapt Tarot magic to match any set of occult correspondences. That is part of its versatility—the cards are moveable and may be set in any desired arrangement. Those interested in my modifications to the Tarot correspondences will find them explained in the appendix.

For many years, I used Tarot magic as part of my own ritual work but did not teach it, or even reduce it to a separate integrated system. In several of my books, I mention it briefly as a subject worth the consideration of serious readers. For example, in my first book, *The New Magus*, published in 1988, I wrote: "The uses of the Tarot in magic are too many to list. Each individual card can be the object of fruitful meditations. Cards can be used as talismans, as instruments of ritual workings, as patterns for godforms, and as symbols of power. Above all else, the Tarot is a tool for examining the Self and its relation to life" (Tyson, 183).

Little did I imagine when I wrote those words that it would be nearly two decades before I would find an opportunity to present the system of Tarot magic that I was then developing and using in my own rituals. Here for the first time, that system is revealed in full detail and in a unified format. Those who master it will find that it frees them from the burden of the complex physical apparatus of traditional ceremonial occultism. I have deliberately restricted the system described here to the cards themselves and only the cards. The goal is simplicity. The Tarot is a symbolic model of the universe. Nothing external to it is required.

Traditional magic relies on symbolism also, but in its often complex and ornate ceremonies these symbols are embodied by physical objects and instruments. For example, the magic circle is a protective shield or barrier that is physically marked or laid out on the floor or ground where the ritual is worked. It is well understood by those skilled in ritual that there is another intangible circle that exists on the astral level in the mind of the magician, without which the physical circle would be powerless. The circle held in the imagination is the living soul of the magic circle, and the physical circle laid out or marked on the floor serves as its body.

It is possible to represent the astral realities of ritual magic with symbolic rather than physical instruments. An astral circle can be grounded or given a body by means of a group of Tarot cards just as effectively as it is grounded by a circle drawn in chalk on the floor. In both cases, it is the circle in the imagination of the magician that is the true working circle of the ritual, but in traditional magic it is fixed in the form of a circle drawn, painted, or otherwise marked on the floor, whereas in Tarot magic it is fixed by means of an arrangement of cards that embodies the ritual circle in its set of esoteric correspondences.

Nor is it necessary to lay the cards out in a large circle within which the magician stands and works. This is one possible use for the cards. I have myself employed it in rituals and it can be effective, but to think only in these terms limits the versatility of Tarot magic. Just as a group of cards can represent the true magic circle on the astral level, so can a single card, carefully chosen, represent and embody the magician. The ring of cards defining the circle need then be only large enough to contain the card of the magician and any other symbolic tools used in the circle. This allows Tarot magic to be worked on a tabletop or similar convenient surface. A ritual chamber is unnecessary because the deck of cards becomes the ritual chamber.

It may seem strange that the magician enters one of the cards during rituals of Tarot magic. In the Western esoteric tradition, it is usual for the magician to remain within his or her own body during the greater part of ritual work. This is not equally so in the magic of the East. Tibetan magicians work with esoteric designs laid out upon the floor or the ground that express in symbolic form astral temples, astral landscapes, or entire planes of being without physical reality. They project themselves into these pictures by identifying themselves with a small token, which they place within the design, usually at its center. As long as the token that embodies their identity remains within the design, they are present and self-aware in the astral reality that the design represents.

The technique of projecting the point of view, or self-awareness, outside the body requires practice, but such projection is an established part of Western magic as well. It is used for a variety of purposes, such as projecting the self-awareness through an astral doorway during scrying or soul flight, or into a godform when invoking a higher spiritual being. It is a technique every person serious about magic must learn sooner or later, and it is not very difficult. Any beginner can project his or her self-awareness to a limited and partial degree, although full perfection of the technique requires months or years of practice. A virtue of Tarot magic is that it can be worked with success even if the projection of the point of view into a card is less than perfect.

This system does not require the purchase of a special Tarot deck. Any Tarot of seventy-eight cards will be effective. The occult correspondences of the Golden Dawn upon which the entire system is based are independent of the details of the card images, so the differences between the Rider-Waite deck and the Crowley Thoth deck, for example, do not determine the success of the magic worked. The magic is not in the cards, which are merely tools used to construct rituals and to represent various instruments and forces. The magic is in the person using them. The cards act to focus and project the power of the mind.

Decks of smaller cards produce a more manageable ritual layout, and are to be preferred in Tarot magic. In my own work, I use the miniature Rider-Waite deck because it can be laid out on a very limited surface area such as a desktop or end table. The size of the cards has no effect on the potency of the magic.

Whichever Tarot deck you select for your own rituals, you should continue to use it until you become completely familiar with its symbolism. Over time, a deck of Tarot cards used repeatedly for ritual magic will acquire its own energies that make it easier to work rituals with that deck. That is because the deck becomes more real on the astral level within the mind of the magician using the cards. Less effort is needed each time by the magician to create the cards on the astral level, freeing up energies for the actual work of magic.

It is best to keep the deck of cards employed in ritual magic separate and wrapped in a square of linen or some other natural cloth, in order to preserve this useful quality of a sustained astral charge. The cards should not be handled by others, or even shown to them. A ritual is a very private activity, unless it is specifically designed to be worked by a group. The tools of ritual are not for curious eyes—the system presented here is intended for the solitary practitioner. Keep the deck separate and use it only for Tarot magic. If you do divination, it is best to get a second deck of cards for that purpose.

Even those who use the Tarot strictly for telling fortunes and have no interest in practical magic will find the explanations for the Golden Dawn Tarot correspondences and their origins more illuminating than any treatment of this subject that has previously appeared in print. For some reason that is not obvious, unless it is mere ignorance on the part of writers, the origin of the Golden Dawn correspondences is seldom adequately explained, though this set of correspondences forms the heart of the modern Tarot. Diviners accept the correspondences without knowing their ultimate source. A full awareness of how the correspondences came to be can enhance the accurate use of the cards for prediction.

This work is solely concerned with practical magic. It is not about using the cards for divination, although this is a fascinating and perfectly valid use for the Tarot. There are thousands of books on fortune telling with the cards, and anyone who seeks to learn to divine will have no trouble finding them. Here, you will discover what is infinitely more rare and precious: a way to use the Tarot ritually to cause active and potent change in the world in conformity with your will. That is the very heart and soul of magic.

2

HISTORY OF THE TAROT

It is only in the past few decades that the origin and history of the Tarot have been known with any degree of assurance. Prior to that time, the wildest rumors circulated in books and among the papers of esoteric organizations. The Tarot was said to be an invention of the Egyptians, or the Hebrews, or the Gypsies. It was said to come from the Middle East, China, or India, or even prehistoric America. It was said to be the inspired teaching of spiritual masters set to watch over and guide the progress of humanity.

Thanks to serious research into the origins of the Tarot that has been done in recent times, we now know that the Tarot was invented in northern Italy in the early part of the fifteenth century, as a card game for the entertainment of noble patrons, and that for centuries it held no recognized occult meaning. The earliest surviving written reference to Tarot cards appeared in 1442. The earliest plausible date for the invention of the Tarot has been given as 1410, with 1425 a more probable year of origin (Decker, Depaulis, and Dummet, *A Wicked Pack of Cards*, 27).

Part of the uncertainty over the date the Tarot was invented stems from the confusion of Tarot cards with ordinary playing cards, which were invented much earlier. Common gaming cards reached Europe from the Middle East around the year 1360, and their origin in the Islamic world is somewhat prior to that. When mention was made of cards in early written records, it was usually to playing cards, but it has often been mistakenly assumed that the references were to Tarot cards, because until quite recently it was thought that the Tarot was older than common cards. The belief was that common cards had descended from the Tarot, whereas we now know that it was the other way around—the Tarot was based in part on playing cards, which were already in wide-

spread use when it was invented.

This confusion caused many writers to date the earliest reference to the Tarot in France as having occurred in the year 1392, when the card maker Jacquemin Gringonneur is recorded to have produced a set of hand-painted cards for King Charles VI. The erroneous assumption was made that these were Tarot cards, and they were associated with an existing partial set of early Tarot cards known, quite incorrectly, as the Charles VI Tarot deck. However, the link had no basis. The Tarot did not become widely known in France until the sixteenth century.

Once it is realized that playing cards were in common use at the time the Tarot was invented, it is easy to see that the suit cards of the Tarot were based on playing cards. The four suits of the Tarot have almost the same structure as the four playing card suits. The major difference is that the Tarot suits have four court cards each, whereas playing card suits have only three court cards. The other difference is in the suit symbols. Playing cards adopted the new suit symbols developed in France around 1470, the familiar Hearts, Diamonds, Spades, and Clubs. Tarot decks continued to use the older suit symbols in use in Europe before the invention of the French suit symbols.

It is less easy to see where the picture cards of the Tarot originated. These twenty-two images have a strange appearance. They seem pregnant with esoteric symbolism, although their exact significance is often in doubt. Some show mythic figures in common use during the early fifteenth century, such as the Fool in his ragged clothes and the dancing goddess of the World. Others, such as the enigmatic Hanged Man, are more distinctive to the Tarot, although it is usually possible to trace their antecedents in earlier woodcuts and paintings.

Compounding the difficulty of understanding the origin of the picture cards is their evolution. The twenty-two images did not remain fixed, but changed over the centuries, and varied from place to place. The structure of the Tarot as a whole was in flux in the early decades of its use for gaming purposes. In some countries the number of cards expanded, while in others it was reduced. Given this mutation of the Tarot, it is surprising how easy it is to recognize Tarot decks, even when there are many variations from what is considered to be the standard deck of seventy-eight cards. While individual cards were added, discarded, or modified, the soul of the Tarot—the essence that gave it a unique, enduring identity—remained intact.

The picture cards did not arise from nothing. In Italy during the early fifteenth century there was a rich artistic tradition concerning emblems—symbolic designs understood to possess a deeper esoteric significance. In literature, the teaching of moral lessons by means of fables was commonplace. Graphic artists extended this practice to pictures, using emblematic symbols for the sake of their simplicity and widespread recognition. Sets of cards arose that are very similar in their general appearance to the picture cards of the Tarot. These cards represented such things as the classical graces, the spheres of the heavens, the virtues, the muses, the classes of human society.

The best example is the set of cards known as the Tarocchi of Mantegna, after the name of the man who was at one time believed to be the artist, Andrea Mantegna of Padua. The actual artist remains unknown, although it may have been Parrasio Michele of Ferrara (Kaplan, *The Encyclopedia of Tarot*, vol. 1, 35). The Mantegna pack is thought to have been engraved around 1470, decades after the invention of the Tarot, and the cards are too large and thin to have been used for gaming, but it shows the tradition of placing symbolic images on cards for the purpose of memorization or instruction that must have existed at the same time the Tarot appeared. The Mantegna pack consists of fifty cards divided into five suits of ten cards, each suit devoted to a different topic: 1–10, the states of mankind; 11–20, Apollo and the muses; 21–30, the liberal arts; 31–40, higher principles; and 41–50, spheres of the universe.

By the year 1781, the early history of the Tarot had long been forgotten, allowing the French Freemason and savant, Antoine Court de Gébelin (1728?–1784), to proclaim in the eighth volume of his nine-volume encyclopedia, *Monde primitif*, that the Tarot had originated as part of the esoteric wisdom tradition of the ancient Egyptians. It was he who derived the meaning of the word Tarot from two supposedly "Oriental" words (*tar* and *rha*) meaning *royal road*.

Around the year 1775, Court de Gébelin arrived at a private party hosted by a woman who had recently returned to France, to find her playing the game of Tarot with friends. After observing the game for a short while, he suddenly declared to everyone present that the card images were allegorical, and furthermore that they had originated in ancient Egypt. In a span of only fifteen minutes, he explained the entire esoteric meaning of the pack, no doubt to the amazement and irritation of those attempting to play the game.

He came up with the theory that the Egyptians had concealed their most important mystery wisdom in a book of cards, by transforming the allegorical knowledge of the book into a card game. His understanding of the esoteric meanings of the Tarot trumps was published three years before his death as part of his enormous, but unfinished, *Monde primitif*. During the following century, the rest of the work was forgotten by posterity, but Court de Gébelin's theories of the Tarot became accepted as fact by many French occultists such as Paul Christian and Eliphas Lévi.

Court de Gébelin found not only an Egyptian origin for the Tarot, but also a Hebrew connection. Lévi and other occultists expanded on this Hebrew source by finding in the structure of the Tarot numerous aspects of the Jewish system of esoteric philosophy known as the Kabbalah. The basis for this historically tenuous connection is the number of the picture cards, twenty-two, which is the same number as the letters of the Hebrew alphabet. Subsequent writers on the Tarot embraced these speculations, elaborating the mystical links between the Tarot and the Egyptian mysteries and Jewish Kabbalah, as well as with the occult traditions of Europe, such as alchemy and astrology.

Shortly after the publication of Court de Gébelin's Tarot theories, the Tarot began to be used for divination. Ordinary playing cards had already been employed for this purpose for some time. Casanova, in his famous *Memoirs*, mentions fortune telling by cards for the year 1765 (Decker, Depaulis, and Dummet, *A Wicked Pack of Cards*, 74). The method witnessed by Casanova probably relied on common cards.

It is possible that Tarot divination predates Court de Gébelin's Tarot essay by a few years. The French card diviner, Etteilla, a seller of seeds and grains by profession whose real name was Jean-Baptiste Alliette (1738–91), included the Tarot in a list of methods of divination in his first book, published in 1770. It is not clear that he knew the method of Tarot divination when he made this list, but in 1782, only one year after the appearance of the speculations of Court de Gébelin, Etteilla attempted to publish a book devoted to Tarot divination. Etteilla is generally known today as a Tarot diviner, but he began his second career as a fortune teller using ordinary playing cards, and probably only moved on to the Tarot after being inspired by Court de Gébelin's essay.

The great French occultists of the nineteenth century were generally less interested in fortune telling with the Tarot than in the mystery tradition of the cards. They used the structure of the cards to elaborate and support various esoteric theories of their own, calling upon the authority of the ancient wisdom that Court de Gébelin had assured them was hidden in the card images. Divination was not ignored, but in the writings of these occultists it was pushed to the background. By the middle of the nineteenth century, Tarot divination was in vogue, and it made prudent sense for any writer to include at least one practical method of Tarot divination amid his more occult speculations on the meaning of the symbolism.

Throughout the nineteenth century, the esoteric Tarot tradition remained largely a French cottage industry. The great savant Court de Gébelin had shown the way, and lesser French luminaries such as Etteilla, Eliphas Lévi (Alphonse-Louis Constant, 1810–75), Paul Christian (Jean-Baptiste Pitois, 1811–77), Stanislas de Guaita (1861–97), and Papus (Gérard-Anaclet-Vincent Encausse, 1865–1916) were content to elaborate on his inspiration. It was only with the founding of the London temple of the Hermetic Order of the Golden Dawn in 1888 that the blossoming esoteric tradition of the Tarot made its way to England, and from there to America.

The Golden Dawn was heavily influenced by the teachings of the French occultists, particularly Eliphas Lévi. Although it pretended to derive its charter from a German Rosicrucian society, its heart was French, as was the wife of its leading member, Samuel L. MacGregor Mathers. Eventually Mathers moved his operations to Paris, completing the circle, but he left a thriving branch of the Golden Dawn behind him in England, and his ties to America remained strong. Mathers further elaborated on Court de Gébelin's teachings, which he regarded as established facts, drawing upon the French occultists for inspiration.

The influence of the Golden Dawn brings us to the present, since it is the system of the Golden Dawn, somewhat modified by members of that Order such as Aleister Crowley and A. E. Waite who disseminated it throughout the world, that is predominant in modern Western esotericism. Here we must stop and think. If it is accepted that the mystery traditions surrounding the Tarot are no more than a fantasy fabricated by Court de Gébelin and elaborated by Lévi, Mathers, Crowley, and others, where does that leave us regarding the use of the Tarot for a system of ritual magic?

Happily, the meaningfulness and effectiveness of the Tarot are not dependent on claims regarding its historical evolution. That power and meaning come from the symbolism of the cards themselves. While it is true that no ancient Hebrew root for the Tarot can be proved, the structure of the Tarot supports an association with aspects of the Kabbalah. The artists who created the Tarot in northern Italy in the early fifteenth century may not have had the Hebrew alphabet in mind when they settled on twenty-two picture cards for the deck, but it cannot be denied that there are twenty-two picture cards, making it natural to associate the picture cards with the Hebrew letters.

Similarly, the images suggest Egyptian, Greek, and biblical mythic elements. This does not support an Egyptian, Greek, or Hebrew source for the Tarot, but it allows the association of the Tarot with certain aspects of these powerful racial currents in the Western esoteric tradition. As a consequence, the Tarot can be used to channel the spiritual and magical energies of these traditions. In its broadest sense, symbolism is not dependent for its meaning on its period and place of origin. It transcends time and place. Tarot symbolism is as potent today as it was when placed on the cards six centuries ago.

The effectiveness of the cards as instruments of divination has been proven countless times over the past two hundred years. Occultists who have studied them are in agreement that they perpetuate in their structure an esoteric model of the universe that has great utility in tying together many diverse threads of magic, myth, and philosophy. It is my own personal assertion, based on three decades of experiment, that the Tarot is equally potent as an instrument of practical ritual magic. It origins, be they ancient or modern, sacred or mundane, cannot diminish the meaning of the cards or deprive them of their power.

3

STRUCTURE OF
THE TAROT

The standard Tarot consists of seventy-eight cards having two main divisions called the Greater Arcana, or trumps, and the Lesser Arcana, or suits. *Arcana* is the plural form of *arcanum*, and simply means mysteries. In the earliest Tarots, neither Roman nor Arabic numerals appeared on any of the cards. The ordering of the trumps of the Greater Arcana was a received tradition that was taught orally but not marked on the trumps. Repetitions of the suit symbol defined the value of each number card of the Lesser Arcana, just as they did in common playing card decks until quite recent times.

The Greater Arcana are the twenty-two picture cards that are usually numbered in traditional decks (prior to the mid-nineteenth century) with Roman numerals. Modern decks (after the mid-nineteenth century) sometimes use Arabic numerals to number the trumps. Each image is completely different from all the others, and each trump has an independent identity that derives from its picture. The Roman numerals are used only to indicate the traditional ordering of the cards when they are considered together as a group. The Roman numerals do not form a part of the essential identity of the trumps.

By contrast, meaning for the number cards of the Lesser Arcana does not derive from their pictures, but from their numbers in the context of their suits, since in traditional Tarot decks the number cards carry no pictorial scenes at all, but only stylized designs composed of the repeated suit symbol. The scenes on the number cards in a modern deck such as the Rider-Waite Tarot express, in a dramatic visual way, the meanings of the cards according to the personal interpretation of the deck designer. It is regrettable that many who use modern decks mistake these interpretive scenes for the primary meanings of the numbered suit cards, rather than basing their understanding on the numbers themselves.

This distinction is essential in understanding the Tarot, and the way in which the cards are used in Tarot magic. The trumps are the unique pictorial scenes they bear; the number cards of the suits are the numbers they bear, expressed through multiples of the suit symbols. Even though the trumps in both traditional and modern decks are usually numbered, those numbers are not an intrinsic part of the essential natures of the trumps. Similarly, even though the numbered suit cards in modern decks bear pictorial scenes, those scenes are not an intrinsic part of the identities of the number cards, but merely interpretations of those identities.

The sixteen court cards of the Lesser Arcana bridge the gulf between the trumps and the number cards, deriving their natures both from the images they bear and from the suits to which they belong. Their images are neither wholly unique, as the images of the trumps are, nor are they strictly repetitive. Each court card depicts a solitary noble figure, either a king, queen, knight, or page, and although each suit contains these four royal ranks, no court card is exactly like any other.

Since the identities of the trumps reside in the images they bear, and these images vary from deck to deck, it follows that the essential natures of the trumps will vary depending on which deck is used. For example, differences in symbolism on the trump the Star between the traditional Marseilles deck and the modern Thoth deck change the very identity of that trump. Over the centuries, a general and somewhat vague consensus has developed as to what symbolism should appear on the trumps, so that they may be recognized, but modern Tarot designers often depart from the traditional images of the trumps in radical ways.

In an attempt to stabilize the meanings of the trumps, and render them to some extent independent of their changeable images, occult schools applied various systems of correspondences to the trumps. These are sets of esoteric symbols that are attached to each trump, and by their association modify and limit the meaning of the trump independent of any pictorial symbolism that appears on the card, or any changes that may be made to existing symbolism. Ideally, the meanings imposed through a system of correspondences will be in harmony with the inherent traditional meanings of the trumps. The most successful system of occult correspondences for the trumps is that developed by the late-nineteenth century English Rosicrucian society, the Hermetic Order of the Golden Dawn, about which more will be written in chapter 4.

The Fool has always been differentiated from the other trumps. In older Tarots where the trumps carry Roman numerals, the Fool alone among the trumps remains unnumbered. It is usually assigned a zero in modern decks, a practice that originated with the teachings of Court de Gébelin and was carried on by the Golden Dawn. For the purposes of Tarot magic, this card should always be understood to carry a zero, even if a zero does not appear on the face of the card in the particular deck chosen. The Fool is located at the beginning of the trumps, just as zero precedes one.

The other trumps are most often given Roman numerals from I to XXI. However, there is no Roman numeral for zero. This practice of leaving the Fool unnumbered or giving it a zero defines a division in the Greater Arcana that has considerable esoteric meaning. The trumps naturally split into two parts—the solitary Fool, and the other twenty-one picture cards. Esoterically, the Fool remains aloof and apart, and for this reason it interacts with all the other trumps equally. The Fool is a kind of touchstone against which the other trumps are contrasted and evaluated.

The fifty-six cards of the Lesser Arcana are divided into four suits in a way similar to ordinary playing cards. Indeed, there can be little doubt that the Lesser Arcana is derived from playing cards, which had been widely employed for gaming purposes in Europe for decades when the Tarot was created in northern Italy in the early part of the fifteenth century. The names for the suits used in this book are Wands, Cups, Swords, and Pentacles. Wands correspond with the playing card suit of Clubs; Cups correspond with Hearts; Swords correspond with Spades; Pentacles correspond with Diamonds.

Even though playing cards are older than Tarot cards, the suit symbols used in the Tarot predate the suit symbols of modern playing cards, which were simplified by French playing card designers to make printing the cards less costly. Originally, playing cards employed the same suit symbols as Tarot cards. Around 1470, half a century or so after the invention of the Tarot, French card makers came up with the modern suit symbols we still use today, and these eventually replaced the older symbols on playing cards throughout most of Europe. Tarot designers were a more conservative group and chose to retain the original symbols.

The details of Tarot suit symbols do not remain absolutely constant throughout their history, but vary from place to place and from deck to deck. These minor differences are reflected in the names given to the symbols. Wands are sometimes called Rods of Staffs. Cups are sometimes called Chalices or Goblets. Swords are sometimes known as Daggers or, more rarely, Pins. Pentacles are also called Disks or Coins. The names for the suits employed here are those used by both the Golden Dawn and by the popular Rider-Waite Tarot.

The essential meaning for a suit symbol resides in its general shape, not in its ornamentation or designation. In a general sense, Wands are wooden rods or staffs that are similarly blunt at both ends. Cups are concave vessels for holding liquids. Swords are steel blades pointed at a single end. Pentacles are flat, circular disks. It is these shapes that must be considered when seeking to understand the overall nature of the suits. Wands express balanced force and rule. Cups express nurture and reflection. Swords express directed force and punishment. Pentacles express solidity and substance.

Each suit contains ten cards numbered from One to Ten. The Ones are often known as Aces. Each suit also holds four noble or court cards generally known as the King, Queen, Knight, and Page. In some esoteric decks these names are altered, but the system of Golden Dawn correspondences used throughout this book is based on the order of the court cards, and remain unchanged regardless of how the cards may be titled, or what specific details of symbolism appear on the cards. The Page has the same associations whether it is called the Knave or the Princess because it is the fourth of the four court cards of its suit. For the sake of familiarity I have used the names for the court cards employed in the popular Rider-Waite Tarot—King, Queen, Knight, and Page.

Why the Tarot has four court cards in each suit, and common playing cards have only three court cards in each suit, remains a mystery. All explanations are conjectural. It used to be widely assumed that the Knights represented court cards that had been lost from common playing decks at some point in their evolution, but now that we know playing cards are older than the Tarot, this explanation seems less plausible. In any case, traditional Italian and Spanish playing card decks contain a King, Knight, and Page in each suit, and omit the Queen, making the question even more obscure.

There is some evidence that at its earliest beginnings the Tarot had not four, but six court cards in each suit, and that subsequently two of them were dropped. In a hand-painted Italian Tarot deck dated around 1441, each suit contains three pairs of court cards: King-Queen, Knight-Dame, and Page-Maid. This may have been part of the original design for the Tarot, but if so, it did not survive more than a few decades, and was quickly replaced with the four court cards in each suit with which we are familiar.

There are ten general groupings of the cards within the body of the Tarot that arise directly from its structure:

1) Greater Arcana

2) Lesser Arcana

3) The Fool

4) Other trumps

5) Suit of Wands

6) Suit of Cups

7) Suit of Swords

8) Suit of Pentacles

9) Number cards

10) Court cards

Numerous additional divisions of the cards into various groups based on interpretations of symbolism or occult associations have been made, but these are not evident in the makeup of the Tarot itself. For example, it is possible to divide the twenty-one trumps other than the Fool into three groups of seven cards each, and the cards within each group of seven might be linked with the seven planets of traditional astrology. However, the symbolism of the trumps does not support such a division.

In Tarot magic, we are concerned only with the ten natural groups founded upon the innate structure of the Tarot, and with the subgroups that arise directly as a result of the Golden Dawn occult correspondences, not with other more speculative groupings of the cards that rely on an intuitive interpretation of Tarot symbolism, or conjectured sets of associations that have not achieved a general consensus in the modern Western tradition.

4

TAROT AND THE
GOLDEN DAWN

Throughout this work you will encounter mentions of the Golden Dawn. It is important to understand its place in the Western esoteric tradition and its influence on the Tarot, since the Golden Dawn set of occult correspondences for the Tarot forms the foundation of Tarot magic. The Golden Dawn system of magic does not contain the system of Tarot magic described in this book, or anything like it, but Tarot magic relies on the Golden Dawn correspondences to support the underlying pattern upon which its basic ritual method is constructed.

The Hermetic Order of the Golden Dawn was a Rosicrucian secret society founded in London in 1888 by three high-ranking Freemasons for the purpose of studying, preserving, teaching, and using the techniques of ritual magic for the greater betterment of mankind. The men and women in its ranks numbered among the leading artists, writers, and social luminaries of England. A few of its members, notably Dion Fortune, Aleister Crowley, and Arthur Edward Waite, went on to establish their own occult schools and spread its various teachings far and wide through their writings after the Order ceased to be active.

It was a daring concept for its time. Although Freemasonry has always contained esoteric symbolism in its rituals and embellishments, it has seldom sought to use the occult wisdom it is reputed to hold for any practical purpose. The founders of the Golden Dawn wished to revive Rosicrucianism as an active esoteric school embracing all the major occult currents of the Western tradition, among them Hermetic philosophy, alchemy, the Tarot, and the Kabbalah, and sought to use these ancient teachings in the daily practice of ceremonial magic. They were bold enough to extend their teachings to both men and women, a practice uncommon in the tradition of Freemasonry.

The three founders were men of curious contrasts. Dr. William Robert Woodman (1828–91) was a senior Freemason of great authority who died shortly after the founding of the Golden Dawn, and so played little part in the development of its system of magic. He possessed a knowledge of Hebrew and the Kabbalah, and may have been in part responsible for the inclusion of the Kabbalah in the magic of the Golden Dawn. The other two remained close friends and worked together for many years. Each brought his unique talents forward in support of the Order. Dr. William Wynn Westcott (1848–1925) was by profession a London coroner. He possessed an extensive knowledge for his day of classical works on Hermetism and Greek philosophy. It is mainly due to his scholarship that the Kabbalah played so important a role in the Golden Dawn. Samuel Liddell Mathers (1854–1918), who called himself "MacGregor" Mathers on the fanciful notion that he was descended from the Scottish royal bloodline, was a diligent seeker after occult manuscripts in the libraries of England and France. He spent much of his time immediately prior to the founding of the Order in the Reading Room of the British Museum, poring over crabbed, handwritten grimoires. It is to Mathers that the Golden Dawn owes its complex symbolic rituals and its eclectic blend of practical magic.

In order to lend the fledgling Golden Dawn the authority of an occult pedigree, Westcott concocted a fictional history that traced the beginnings of the Golden Dawn to the German occult society *Die Goldene Dämmerung*. Supposedly, the charter for the Golden Dawn was given to Westcott by a certain Fräulein Sprengel, head of an apocryphal German branch of the Golden Dawn, which claimed to be in direct contact with the spiritual teachers of Rosicrucianism. It did not hurt this fictional history that Rosicrucianism had its birth in Germany. For years, this ploy of Westcott's worked, but eventually the truth became known, and played a large part in the decline of the original Golden Dawn.

The history of the Order presented to members at the time of their initiation may have been merely a fiction designed to lend it a greater authority, but the system of magic it taught was firmly based on the magical methods of the Renaissance supplemented by the more recent teachings of French occultists of the nineteenth century, most notable among them Eliphas Lévi. Had this been the only sources of its teachings, the Golden Dawn might have remained merely a curious social club for antiquarians of the occult, but the synthesis of its teachings was the result of psychic communications from a group of spiritual beings known as the Secret Chiefs.

The human Chiefs of the Order were the three Freemasons who founded it. The Secret Chiefs were three very powerful and wise spiritual beings of the Rosicrucian occult current whose names were given in the Adeptus Minor Ritual of the Golden Dawn as:

> Frater Hugo Alverda, the Phrisian, in the 576th year of his age.
> Frater Franciscus de Bry, the Gaul, in the 495th year of his age.
> Frater Elman Zata, the Arab, in the 463rd year of his age.
>
> (Regardie, *The Golden Dawn*, 6th ed., 237)

It is not clear whether these spiritual teachers and leaders possessed bodies of deathless flesh, or bodies of eternal spirit, but they were considered so powerful and so exalted that the distinction between spirit and flesh held little meaning.

Samuel L. "MacGregor" Mathers was a psychic of considerable ability. His wife Moïna, formerly Mina Bergson, the beautiful sister of the French philosopher Henri Bergson, was also psychic, and assisted him in receiving and recording the teachings of the Secret Chiefs. These teachings consisted of a set of complex initiation rituals and a detailed system of occultism that constituted the Second Order of the Golden Dawn, where ceremonial magic was the primary practice.

Mathers described the way in which he communicated with the Secret Chiefs in a letter written in 1896, though it is not clear whether the three Chiefs named in the Adeptus Minor Ritual are intended, or other exalted teachers, since Mathers confessed that he himself did not know their names.

> Concerning the Secret Chiefs of the Order, to whom I make reference and from whom I have received the Wisdom of the Second Order which I have communicated to you, I can tell you *nothing*.
>
> I do not even know their earthly names.
>
> I know them only by certain secret mottoes.
>
> I have *but very rarely* seen them in the physical body; and on such rare occasions *the rendezvous was made astrally by them* at the time and place which had been astrally appointed beforehand.
>
> For my part I believe them to be human and living upon this earth; but possessing terrible superhuman powers.
>
> When such rendezvous has been in a much frequented place, there has been nothing in their personal appearance and dress to mark them out as differing in any way from ordinary people except the appearance and sensation of transcendent health and physical vigour (whether they seemed persons in youth or age) which was their invariable accompaniment; in other words, the physical appearance which the possession of the Elixir of Life has traditionally supposed to confer.
>
> (Howe, *Magicians of the Golden Dawn*, 129–30)

Concerning the role of his wife, Moïna, in the reception of the occult teachings of the Secret Chiefs, Mathers revealed that he had specifically asked the Secret Chiefs that she be permitted to help him in his work, presumably because she possessed psychic gifts that he found quite useful. She was known in the Golden Dawn by her Latin motto Soror Vestigia Nulla Retrorsum, or on a more familiar level simply as Vestigia. Mathers wrote: "At my urgent request, Soror Vestigia Nulla Retrorsum was allowed to be associated with me in this labour, but only on condition of pledging herself in the same manner, though in a less degree" (Howe, 128). The pledge mentioned by Mathers consisted mainly in doing whatever the Secret Chiefs demanded without question, and also remaining pure—that is, refraining from sexual intercourse or sexual orgasm—in order to increase the vital energy of the body.

In addition to direct contact with the Secret Chiefs, both on the physical and the astral planes, Mathers and his wife had recourse to the usual techniques of nineteenth century spiritualism to obtain their spirit communications. Mathers mentions the "table" as well as "the ring and the disc." The table is probably communication by means of rapping noises from a wooden table during seances, a common method. One rap signified yes, two raps no, and the medium could specify to the spirit the meaning of various numbers or combinations of raps to achieve more complex responses. The ring and the disc is a method of divination by which a ring is suspended on a length of silk thread over a disk of paper *pendulum* marked with a cross. The swing of the ring in ways agreed on beforehand with the spirits in control of the ring was accepted as either a positive or a negative response. For example, the swing of the ring in an arc above the vertical arm of the cross might be interpreted as a yes, and the swing of the ring above the horizontal arm taken as a no to any question put to the spirits.

Mathers also mentions in passing the use of ritual evocation as part of his communication with the Secret Chiefs. This is the calling of spirits to be present in tangible form, so that they may better interact with the magician who summons them. Mathers was a skilled practitioner of spirit evocation, so much so that his black sheep of a student, Aleister Crowley, continued to regard Mathers as a powerful magician long after he had lost faith in Mathers in every other way.

Part of the system of magic delivered to MacGregor Mathers by the incorporeal beings he referred to as the Secret Chiefs was an original set of designs for the Tarot, along with a set of esoteric associations or correspondences for the cards. Moïna Mathers was a skilled artist. The reason she had traveled from France to London was to sketch in the British Museum, where Mathers first encountered her. She painted the cards of the Golden Dawn Tarot herself. After the dissolution of the original Golden Dawn, her Tarot deck appears to have been hidden, lost, or destroyed. Partial descriptions of the cards survived in the documents of the Order, and from these descriptions the Golden Dawn Tarot has been re-created. The best attempt is that of Sandra Tabatha Cicero (*The New Golden Dawn Ritual Tarot*, Llewellyn, 1991).

We are concerned here not with the Tarot painted by Moïna Mathers, but with the esoteric correspondences assigned to the cards by MacGregor Mathers, based on the psychic communications he and his wife received from the Secret Chiefs. These correspondences form the basis for the standard interpretation of the cards of the modern Tarot. Other systems of correspondences exist, but none is so widely accepted or so rational as that of the Golden Dawn.

Commenting upon the correspondences for the Tarot that he received from the spirits presiding over the Golden Dawn, Mac-Gregor Mathers wrote at the end of the Tarot document known as *Book T*: "In all of this I have not only transcribed the symbolism, but have tested, studied, compared, and examined it both clairvoyantly and in other ways. The result of these has been to show me how *absolutely* correct the symbolism of the Book T is, and how exactly it represents the occult Forces of the Universe" (Regardie, *The Golden Dawn*, 6th ed., 565).

It is important to establish here explicitly that the Golden Dawn Tarot correspondences were transmitted to Mathers from spiritual intelligences of a higher order, because this is the manner in which all significant seminal teachings in the Western occult tradition are conveyed into the world. Such wisdom always has a spiritual source. Living systems of magic, those possessing power and effectiveness for those who work them, are never invented in an arbitrary way, but are invariably received from spirit teachers by psychic means, or based upon that received wisdom.

My own system of Tarot magic is founded upon the Golden Dawn correspondences. Since it is drawn from the teachings of the Golden Dawn, Tarot magic and Golden Dawn magic are in perfect

channeled/ downloaded

harmony—useful because the Golden Dawn system of ritual magic is the most widely accepted form of magic in the Western world. Many who work magic are not aware that the techniques they use are derived from the Golden Dawn teachings, but they owe a huge debt to MacGregor Mathers and his wife for their years of selfless psychic labor, and to the higher spiritual beings known as the Secret Chiefs who instructed them.

5

CORRESPONDENCES
OF THE TRUMPS

In the Tarot correspondences of the Golden Dawn, the twenty-two
cards of the Greater Arcana are linked with the twenty-two letters
of the Hebrew alphabet. The Hebrew letters need not concern us
too much since they are not required for Tarot magic, but it is necessary to know about this connection of the trumps with the letters, because it is through the esoteric attributions given to the Hebrew letters in the Kabbalah that the trumps derive their most
important associations.

The Hebrew alphabet is divided by Kabbalists into three groups
known as the Mother letters, the Double letters, and the Single (or
Simple) letters. "Twenty-two are the Letters, the Foundation of all
things; there are Three Mothers, Seven Double and Twelve Simple letters" (Westcott, *Sepher Yetzirah*, 15). These terms are based
on the sounds of the letters. It was believed that the sounds of the
Mother letters gave rise to all the other letter sounds. The Double
letters are sometimes said to be those letters that are sounded two
ways, and the Single letters are those sounded only one way.

The three Mother letters are linked in the Kabbalah with higher
or active aspects of the three elements: Fire, Air, and Water. The
seven Double letters are linked with the seven planets of traditional
astrology: Saturn, Jupiter, Mars, the Sun, Venus, Mercury, and the
Moon. The twelve Single letters are linked with the twelve signs of

the zodiac: Aries, Taurus, Gemini, Cancer, Leo, Virgo, Libra, Scorpio, Sagittarius, Capricorn, Aquarius, and Pisces.

These assignments to the groups of Hebrew letters are based on the authority of the most ancient and revered of all Kabbalistic texts, *Sepher Yetzirah* (*Book of Formation*), which one of the mortal Chiefs of the Golden Dawn, Wynn Westcott, translated into English from various sources and caused to be published in 1887. It is not known how old this text is, but the noted Kabbalistic scholar Gershom Scholem dated it as early as the second century (Scholem, *Kabbalah*, 26).

No mention is made in *Sepher Yetzirah*, nor in any other traditional Kabbalistic document, of the Tarot. Only after Court de Gébelin pointed out in 1781 that the number of trumps matched the number of Hebrew letters did occultists attempt to integrate the Tarot and the Kabbalah by using the Hebrew alphabet as a kind of glue. In the Golden Dawn correspondences, the Tarot trumps are aligned with the Hebrew letters in a direct one-to-one relationship, the first trump with the first letter, the second trump with the second letter, and so on. Since Mathers placed the Fool at the head of the trumps, after the example of Court de Gébelin and Eliphas Lévi, it received the first Hebrew letter, Aleph.

It is essential to understand that the elemental and astrological factors in the Tarot correspondences are attributed primarily to the three groups of Hebrew letters rather than to the trumps. Across the bridge of the Hebrew alphabet, these elemental and astrological factors became associated in a secondary way with the trumps. It is with these secondary associations that we are concerned in Tarot magic, not with the Hebrew alphabet itself. Each trump embodies and expresses the elemental or astrological quality to which it is linked. By manipulating the trump in ritual, we can manipulate that energy.

The third chapter of *Sepher Yetzirah* concerns the three Mother letters, where it is written:

He [God] caused the letter Aleph to reign in Air and crowned it, and combining it with the others He sealed it, as Air in the World, as the temperate (climate) of the Year, and as the breath in the chest (the lungs for breathing air) in Man: the male with Aleph, Mem, Shin, the female with Shin, Mem, Aleph. He caused the letter Mem to reign in Water, crowned it, and combining it with the others formed the earth in the world, cold in the year, and the belly in man, male and female, the former with Mem, Aleph, Shin, the latter with Mem, Shin, Aleph. He caused Shin to reign in Fire, and crowned it, and combining it with the others sealed with it the heavens in the universe, heat in the year and the head in man, male and female.

(Westcott, *Sepher Yetzirah*, 21)

The links between the Mother letters and the three active elements are explicit and can give rise to no confusion. Mathers was able to place the active elements on the Tarot trumps with confidence. When the text of *Sepher Yetzirah* moves on to the seven Double letters and the assignment of the planets, the exact placement of the planets on the letters is not made clear. It was for this crucial information that Mathers relied on the communications of the Secret Chiefs. The relevant text in the fourth chapter of *Sepher Yetzirah* reads:

These Seven Double Letters He designed, produced, and combined, and formed with them the Planets of this World, the Days of the Week, and the Gates of the soul (the orifices of perception) in Man. . . . So now, behold the Stars of our World, the Planets, which are Seven; the Sun, Venus, Mercury, Moon, Saturn, Jupiter and Mars.

(Westcott, *Sepher Yetzirah*, 23)

It might be assumed that this list of planets is to be assigned to the Double letters in its order, but it has another hidden purpose. It is intended to illustrate to the initiated the relationship between the natural order of the planets and the order of the seven days of the week, to each of which is assigned one of the planets. The natural order of the planets is based on their apparent speeds of motion across the heavens. From quickest to slowest, it is Moon,

Planets on the Heptagram

Mercury, Venus, Sun, Mars, Jupiter, Saturn. The order of the planets on the days of the week is Sun (Sunday), Moon (Monday), Mars (Tuesday), Mercury (Wednesday), Jupiter (Thursday), Venus (Friday), and Saturn (Saturday).

There is a very elegant graphic symbol, the unicursal heptagram, which beautifully illustrates this relationship, and the author of *Sepher Yetzirah* deliberately evoked this symbol by the particular order he gave to the planets in his list, while taking care to in no way explicitly indicate the construction of the symbol, which must have been secret knowledge.

Aleister Crowley learned about the arrangement of the planets on the points of the heptagram from his teacher, MacGregor Mathers, who probably came to an inspired understanding of it while studying Westcott's edition of *Sepher Yetzirah*. Crowley was greatly impressed by this figure, as well he should have been. In my opinion, it may be the basis for the ordering of our days of the week.

If you look at the list of the seven planets given in *Sepher Yetzirah*, and place them in this order in a circle around the points of the heptagram counterclockwise, you will see that the natural ordering of the planets by their speeds of motion across the heavens is presented when you start with the Moon (the quickest) and move in a circle around the heptagram in a clockwise direction. However, if you follow the recrossing line of the heptagram from point to point in a counterclockwise direction, beginning with the point of the Sun (Sunday), you will get the ordering of the planets on the days of the week.

As beautiful as this arrangement of the planets on the points of the heptagram may be, it does not indicate the correct placement of the planets on the seven Double letters. In a note on this question, Wynn Westcott wrote:

> In associating the particular letters to each planet, the learned Jesuit Athanasius Kircher allots Beth to the Sun, Gimel to Venus, Daleth to Mercury, Kaph to Luna, Peh to Saturn, Resh to Jupiter, and Tau to Mars. Kalisch in the supplementary paragraphs gives a different attribution; both are wrong, according to clairvoyant investigation. Consult the Tarot symbolism given by Court de Gébelin, Eliphas Lévi, and my notes to the *Isiac Tablet of Bembo*. The true attribution is probably not anywhere printed.
>
> (Westcott, *Sepher Yetzirah*, 46)

Westcott was being rather daring in making veiled reference to the Tarot when commenting in his note on the correct arrangement of the seven planets on the Double letters, since this arrangement, which he does not reveal, was undoubtedly a secret communicated to him by Mathers, and not intended for the ears or eyes of the uninitiated. Westcott's edition of *Sepher Yetzirah* was published one year before the establishment of the Hermetic Order of the Golden Dawn, so it is evident that Mathers psychically received the ordering of the planets on the Double letters before the founding of the Golden Dawn, but probably not much prior to its founding.

The placement of the signs of the zodiac on the twelve Single letters is also concealed in *Sepher Yetzirah*, but not deeply, and it is possible to be fairly sure about the attribution. The relevant text of the fifth chapter reads:

> The Twelve Simple Letters are Heh, Vau, Zain, Cheth, Teth, Yod, Lamed, Nun, Samech, Oin, Tzaddi and Qoph. . . . These Twelve Simple Letters He designed, and combined, and formed with them the Twelve celestial constellations of the Zodiac, whose signs are Teth, Shin, Tau, Samech, Aleph, Beth, Mem, Oin, Qoph, Gimel, Daleth and Daleth.
>
> (Westcott, *Sepher Yetzirah*, 25)

These two lists of letters might give brief pause to the understanding, but there is no deep mystery here. The first list is the Simple letters in their natural order in the Hebrew alphabet. The second list appears obscure, but it is the initial letters in the Hebrew names of the zodiac signs in their natural order beginning with Aries. The signs of the zodiac are to be placed on the Single letters in their usual sequence. Of course, it is remotely possible that the author of *Sepher Yetzirah* did not intend that a direct assignment be made between the Simple letters and the signs, but later commentators assumed a direct relationship, and Mathers and Westcott agreed with them.

There is no necessity to understand how the Golden Dawn Tarot correspondences for the trumps were derived in order to work Tarot magic, but it is useful to know that they are based in the earliest history of the Kabbalah. Mathers's contribution to this ancient core of the correspondences was the psychically directed placement of the planets on the Double letters, and also the assignment of the individual trumps to the Hebrew alphabet. In the Golden Dawn Tarot, the trumps Justice and Strength trade positions from those they occupy in the traditional Tarot.

This change to the traditional order of the trumps was made by Mathers to better make the trumps harmonize with the zodiac signs of the Hebrew letters linked to these cards. When a one-to-one link is made between the trumps in their traditional order with the Fool at the beginning (after the practice of Eliphas Lévi) and the Hebrew letters in their natural order, it is found that the trump Justice receives the zodiac sign of Leo, the Lion, and the trump Strength receives the zodiac sign of Libra, the Scales. However, on the face of the trump Justice is depicted a scale, and on the face of the trump Strength is a lion. This was to Mathers an obvious indication that these trumps must be inverted in their placements in the sequence of the Greater Arcana.

Below are the correspondences of the Golden Dawn between the trumps and the elements, planets, and signs. Some of the names of the trumps are shortened forms of those commonly used in modern Tarot decks. There are sometimes variant titles for the trumps, but these should not create confusion. For example, the Magician is also called the Magus or Juggler in some decks. The World is sometimes known as the Universe. The Hierophant is called the Pope in older decks, and the High Priestess is known as the Female Pope or Papess. For the purpose of Tarot magic, it is immaterial what titles the trumps bear.

Aleph (Mother)	0 Fool–Air
Beth (Double)	I Magician–Mercury
Gimel (Double)	II High Priestess–Moon
Daleth (Double)	III Empress–Venus
Heh (Single)	IV Emperor–Aries
Vau (Single)	V Hierophant–Taurus
Zayin (Single)	VI Lovers–Gemini
Cheth (Single)	VII Chariot–Cancer
Teth (Single)	VIII Strength–Leo
Yod (Single)	IX Hermit–Virgo
Kaph (Double)	X Wheel–Jupiter
Lamed (Single)	XI Justice–Libra
Mem (Mother)	XII Hanged Man–Water
Nun (Single)	XIII Death–Scorpio
Samekh (Single)	XIV Temperance–Sagittarius
Ayin (Single)	XV Devil–Capricorn
Pe (Double)	XVI Tower–Mars
Tzaddi (Single)	XVII Star–Aquarius
Qoph (Single)	XVIII Moon–Pisces
Resh (Double)	XIX Sun–Sun
Shin (Mother)	XX Last Judgment–Fire
Tau (Double)	XXI World–Saturn

[handwritten annotation:]

Most active/potent

Hanged Man
Fool
Judgement
High Priestess
Magician
Empress
Sun
Tower
Wheel
World

All Others (↑)

This set of correspondences has stood the test of time, and has much to recommend it. I have no hesitation in using it as the foundation for Tarot magic since I believe that it is, in the main, correct. However, it should not be regarded as perfect or unchangeable. Aleister Crowley did not think it so, even though he accepted the teachings of the Golden Dawn as a received higher wisdom. In his own work on the Tarot, *The Book of Thoth*, he made an inversion of the associations of the trump the Star with those of the trump the Emperor, to correct what he perceived as an imbalance in the Golden Dawn arrangement of correspondences. He did not take this step on his own authority, but followed the directive of his holy guardian angel, Aiwass, who made the statement in a work psychically received from the spirit by Crowley that "Tzaddi is not the Star" (see Crowley, *The Book of Thoth*, 9; also his *The Book of the Law*, 26).

Crowley would never have taken such a step without higher spiritual direction. He knew that the Secret Chiefs of the Golden Dawn had confirmed Mathers's Tarot correspondences. Only the direct statement by Aiwass that one of these correspondences was incorrect carried enough persuasive force to compel Crowley to reluctantly make his inversion of the associations for the Star and the Emperor. After he studied the change, Crowley came to embrace it with enthusiasm.

In my opinion, Crowley's change has not withstood the test of time. I reject it. However, I believe that the Golden Dawn arrangement, though workable from the standpoint of practical magic, is also imperfect. I will not give my personal amendments to the Golden Dawn correspondences in the body of the text of this book, because I do not wish to confuse readers. It is best to learn the Golden Dawn system before departing from it. All the descriptions and examples in the text are based on the Golden Dawn Tarot correspondences. However, as a matter of interest, I have included my amendments to the correspondences in the appendix, along with my reasons for making them. Those who wish to do so may use these altered correspondences in their own Tarot magic.

6

ESOTERIC COSMOLOGY
OF THE TRUMPS

The Greater Arcana represent spiritual forces and archetypal principles that originate above the material world of cause and effect that is the everyday environment of humanity consciousness. This distinction is not obvious at first glance since almost all the trumps bear human figures, which would seem to integrate them with the common reality of human existence. It is true that the archetypal energies of the trumps express themselves in our daily lives. If they did not, we would have little interest in them. However, those influences are projected from higher levels into our ordinary consciousness, where we become aware of their presence in the form of insights, inspirations, resolves, yearnings, impulses, obsessions, and various types of gnosis.

There is a tangible difference between the quality of our mundane existence and these projected influences that have the power to profoundly change our beliefs and behavior. Anything that arises within us and moves us strongly, yet is difficult to put into words that would explain or justify it, is apt to be a projection from the levels of consciousness represented by the trumps.

The archetypal nature of the trumps is expressed by the Golden Dawn elemental and astrological correspondences that are attached to them. All of the correspondences are to be found in the spherical zones that surround the fixed Earth in the classical, medieval, and Renaissance geocentric models of the universe. The zones have been depicted and labeled by numerous occult philosophers, most notably by Robert Fludd (1574–1637), who had many detailed engravings made of the heavenly spheres, but the same arrangement shown in the illustration on page 41 appears in manuscripts of the twelfth century.

It was believed that the Earth was the unmoving center of the universe around which everything else revolved. Usually it was illustrated as a flat disk or as a square divided into four parts, to correspond with the four lower or material elements and the related four directions. Encircling it were thought to be three elemental zones, the lowest of Water, the middle of Air, and the highest of Fire. These three elemental zones are the higher or more spiritual expression of the three active elements—those elements having motion of their own. The fourth element, Earth, was considered inert because it does not move, change, or flow, and was located on the stable ground that was conceived to be the fixed center of everything.

How the ancients came to this understanding of the elements becomes clear when we consider the physical substances that bear their names. The nature of elemental Earth is well expressed by a stone. Wherever a stone is placed, it remains. There is no motion within the stone itself, so it never tends to flow or drift or roll away unless acted upon by some outside force. When water is poured over a stone, it fails to penetrate the stone, but pools around it, leaving the stone at the center so that the water forms a ring around the stone—the stone penetrates the water, but the water does not penetrate the stone.

The water moves along the surface of the ground unless contained, but does not move upward from the ground. The wind has no such limitation. It is wholly above the surface of the stone and above the water, surrounding and arching over both, yet does not penetrate the water or the stone. When a flame is lit, it attempts to dart upward, ascending through the air in an effort to find a higher vantage. Fire does not wish to remain in air, but wishes to rise above it. It is apparent that as wind is more active in motion than water, so is flame more active than wind. When these four materials are brought together, flame darts upward and water falls downward through the median air, while the stone remains immobile at the base of everything.

The trumps express only higher forces, which in the ancient model of the universe are represented by spheres above the surface of the ground. Since the inert element Earth was not assigned an active form or a zone above the level of the earthly sphere in this cosmology, it is absent from the trumps. The lower, material aspects of all four elements are to be found within the fixed realm of the Earth. We will examine these lower forms of the elements in connection with the four suits of the Lesser Arcana. It is important to understand that the three active spiritual elements corresponding with the three trumps of the Hebrew Mother letters are not quite the same thing as the three out of the four lower material elements that bear the same names.

The members of the Golden Dawn may not have understood why elemental Earth must be omitted from the Hebrew letters, and consequently from the trumps of the Tarot. They made an attempt to slip elemental Earth into the Greater Arcana correspondences through the back door, as it were, by creating a dual association for the final trump, the World. In most tables of the correspondences based on *Sepher Yetzirah* and confirmed by the Secret Chiefs, the World receives only the planet Saturn, but in some documents of the Golden Dawn where the correspondences are shown (Regardie, *The Golden Dawn*, 6th ed., 651), and in similar documents of Aleister Crowley (*The Book of Thoth*, 278), the World is also given elemental Earth.

It is convenient to assign elemental Earth to one of the trumps, from a purely practical standpoint. However, it is contrary to the system of correspondences set forth in *Sepher Yetzirah*, where only three elements are linked with the Hebrew letters, not four. The Golden Dawn members may not have fully grasped that the trumps relate to the active spheres above the fixed realm of the four lower elements, and hence are distinct from the earthly sphere. Elemental Earth simply does not belong among the trumps. On the other hand, it may be that in assigning elemental Earth to the trump the World, Mathers wished to suggest the transition between the lower end of the Greater Arcana and the upper beginning of the Lesser Arcana—between the heavenly spheres and the earthly realm.

The accompanying diagram is a simplification of the cosmology of the heavenly spheres. Those angelic and divine spheres thought to exist above the zone of the zodiac need not concern us since they play no direct part in Tarot magic. Robert Fludd numbered the spheres at twenty-two, to correspond with the twenty-two Hebrew letters. In Fludd's Christian model of the universe, the entire zodiac only gets one letter, and the remaining letters are allotted to higher spheres of the various choirs of angels and God, but in the Kabbalistic model of the universe described in *Sepher Yetzirah*, which we are using and which was used by the Golden Dawn, each zodiac sign is assigned a letter.

The zone of elemental Water immediately around the dry ground of the world was conceived to be very close to the Earth and friendly to it by nature, so that it was sometimes illustrated as a narrow river wrapping around the plain of the world like the body of a sea serpent. That it also existed above the Earth to a limited degree could not be disputed since it is manifest that rain falls from the heavens. Arching over the ground and the ocean was the zone of elemental Air. Hidden from sight above the airy sphere was a zone of rarefied elemental Fire. Fire was understood to be highest of the three active elements because Fire is the lightest and quickest, Air is next in density and motion, and Water is the heaviest and slowest of the three.

Above the three bands of the active elements that surround the unmoving earthly realm are the seven bands of the astrological planets, nesting one inside the other. These circular bands are best conceived as transparent spheres, but are represented in two dimensions as rings in ancient drawings and woodcuts of the cosmos. From the lowest to the highest, they are the spheres of the Moon, Mercury, Venus, the Sun, Mars, Jupiter, and Saturn.

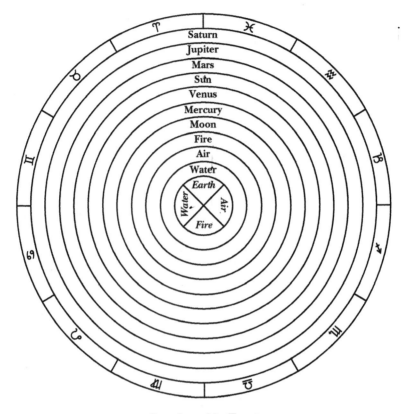

Cosmology of the Trumps

No other planets were known before the time of telescopes. It is just barely possible to see the planet Uranus with the naked eye, but ancient astronomers did not notice it due to its faintness and slow movement, and so remained ignorant of its existence. Neptune and Pluto cannot be seen without the aid of magnifying instruments. The Moon and the Sun are not considered planets today, but in traditional astrology they are classed among the seven wandering bodies, or planets. The Moon was known as the gatekeeper of the heavens because it marks the transition between the lower spheres of the elements and the higher spheres of the planets.

Above the sphere of Saturn, the outermost sphere of the planets, loomed the sphere of the fixed stars. The stars were called fixed by astrologers since on casual inspection they do not appear to change from night to night, but form a backdrop upon which the seven wandering bodies independently move. If you go outside on consecutive nights and look up at the same place in the sky at the same time, you will see that the planets have shifted against the backdrop of the stars and in relation to each other, but that the pattern of stars remains unchanged.

All twelve astrological signs are part of this sphere of the fixed stars. The signs are not constellations but zones of the heavens that bear only a remote connection with the constellations of the same names. They are located in a narrow strip called the zodiac along the plane of the ecliptic, which is the imaginary circle in the sky traced by the apparent path of the Sun. The signs do not get their own spheres, but divide the single sphere of the fixed stars into twelve zones along the band of the zodiac, which extends nine degrees of arc above and nine degrees below the ecliptic. They have their own established order counterclockwise around the girdling band of this starry sphere, which is: Aries, Taurus, Gemini, Cancer, Leo, Virgo, Libra, Scorpio, Sagittarius, Capricorn, Aquarius, and Pisces.

The heavenly spheres nearer the Earth were observed to move more rapidly than those farther from the Earth. This was deduced by recording the speeds of the planets, which were believed to be carried along in their courses by the turning of the transparent spheres in which they were set. The motion slows as we go outward, until, when we reach the fixed stars, the motion almost ceases. Ancient astrologers noticed that the sphere of the fixed stars does indeed move, but it moves very slowly. The star motion, known as the precession of the equinoxes, takes approximately 25,500 years for a single revolution around the heavens.

Consequently, the most active and forceful of the trumps in works of magic are the three linked to the Mother letters, and to the zones of the active elements Water, Air, and Fire that are nearest the central earthly realm. These three trumps are more physically potent and their action more manifest because the spheres with which they are linked lie nearer the tangible Earth, and acquire solidity and force from this proximity. In Tarot magic, the elemental trumps are used to form a gateway through which to bring about the realization of the ritual purpose.

The next most active zones are the seven spheres of the planets, and for this reason the trumps of the Double letters that are associated with these spheres follow in potency or effectiveness in works of magic. Their active energy is not at an equal level, but diminishes with the distance of their spheres from the earthly realm. The trump linked to the sphere of the Moon is most active, and the trump linked with the sphere of Saturn least active among the planetary trumps. The Moon completes her cycle against the backdrop of the stars (a sidereal month) in slightly less than twenty-eight days, whereas Saturn requires more than twenty-nine years for a single orbit. The astrological periods of the planets suggest the relative activity of the trumps to which they are linked.

The twelve trumps associated with the zodiac signs have the lowest active energy, having the least motion about the center. As the signs are all of equal distance from the center, the trumps linked to them are equal in their potency, although they express themselves in different ways. They serve as a backdrop or context for the planetary trumps. During a ritual, the planetary trumps interact with the zodiacal trumps, and by this interaction modify the outcome of the ritual. Although the zodiacal trumps cannot easily be used to initiate change by themselves, because they are relatively motionless, they are useful in shaping and directing the forces of the planetary trumps into desired channels.

7

CORRESPONDENCES
OF THE SUITS

Below the lowest of the ever-restless spheres, that of the active expression of elemental Water, lies the fixed realm of Earth, and it is within the earthly realm that all the cards of the Lesser Arcana find their manifest action. These cards also have a higher spiritual aspect, since everything that exists has both a spiritual and a mundane nature, but in Tarot magic the cards of the Lesser Arcana serve as the workhorses. Whereas the archetypal Greater Arcana cards are employed to shape and define the general ritual structure through which the specific purposes of Tarot magic are achieved, and are therefore independent of particular human desires, the suit cards are the practical vessels that convey the ever-changing intentions of the will. They are used to embody the purposes of a ritual and express its desired outcome.

The four suits represent the four lower or manifest expressions of the elements. You should not mistake the manifest working of the elements for the material substances that give them their names. Even though the lower elements function in the earthly realm, they are much more subtle than physical things. For example, celestial Fire corresponding with the zone of Fire above the earthly realm is extremely rarefied and pure, the intellectual concept of the Fire element; earthly elemental Fire corresponding in the Golden Dawn system with the southern part of the earthly realm is more defined and explicit, the shape and texture of the element. Neither of these is physical fire that burns, although both higher forms of the element Fire are embodied in physical fire. We are dealing with the ideal essence of Fire, the structured conception of Fire, and the material action of Fire when we consider these three levels of the Fire element. The same three levels may be applied to the other elements.

The term *element* is not used in magic as it is used in modern science. For the ancients, everything in the universe was made up of four principles that they called elements. The substances they observed in the natural world that best corresponded with these principles were fire, water, air, and earth. From these physical substances the philosophical elements took their names.

Within the fixed realm of the Earth reside the four lower expressions of the elements Fire, Water, Air, and Earth. Just as the spheres of the higher forms of Fire, Water, and Air are the ideals of the lower forms of these elements, the sphere of the Earth as a whole is the ideal expression of lower elemental Earth. But that ideal of Earth is so dense and inert, it is scarcely to be distinguished from the lower form of elemental Earth, so that the two are, practically speaking, one. It is in this sense that Earth cannot be said to possess a higher expression, and so lacks a celestial sphere of its own.

Wands represent elemental Fire within the earthly realm; Cups stand for elemental Water; Swords for elemental Air; and Pentacles for elemental Earth.

> **Fire** (Warm and Dry) expresses the action of the will. It is hot, explosive, and consuming. It leaps over obstacles and burns up anything that gets in its way. From it the suit of Wands acquires qualities that express themselves through the microcosm or human nature as willfulness, anger, arrogance, inspiration, and aggression.

> **Water** (Cool and Moist) expresses the action of the emotions. It is flowing, cooling, heavy but not hard, permeable, able to take any shape and reflect any image. From it the suit of Cups acquires the qualities in human nature of love, sensitivity, compassion, intuition, empathy, dreaminess, and fantasizing.

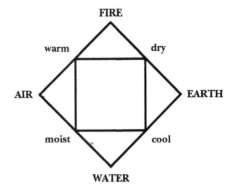

The Four Elements

Air (Warm and Moist) expresses the action of articulate thought. It is quick in its motions, changeable, inconstant, blustery, transparent, light, and warm or cold by turns. From it the suit of Swords takes on the qualities in human nature of perceptiveness, analysis, calculation, rumination, planning, eloquence, persuasiveness, deception, and criticism.

Earth (Cool and Dry) expresses the action of the body. It is heavy, solid, physical, rough, and resistant to change. From it the suit of Pentacles derives the qualities in human nature of physical sensations, strength, endurance, growth, and healthfulness or sickness.

The four suits of the Tarot carry symbols that represent and help to define them:

The suit of Wands has for its symbol a rod or scepter, which indicates authority or rule over others. There is an aristocratic aspect to this suit causing it to stand for the rulers and governors. Traditionally, the nobility.

The suit of Cups is represented by a vessel that sometimes resembles a chalice. From this the suit takes on religious associations of charity and love. It is the suit of the caregivers. Traditionally, the priesthood.

The suit of Swords has as its symbol a sword or dagger, and thus is strongly colored by the associations of warfare and strife. This is the suit of the military and police. Traditionally, the warriors.

The suit of Pentacles is represented by a flat disk that resembles a coin, and indeed in early decks the suit symbol was often a coin. For this reason Pentacles is strongly linked with commerce, trade, business, and money. It is the suit of laborers and those in business. Traditionally, the peasants.

Each suit carries a two-fold general meaning, half of which is based on its associated element, and half based on its symbol.

Wands: will/rule

Cups: emotion/love

Swords: thought/strife

Pentacles: sensation/toil

The suit of Wands is used to dominate or control others, to bring about a willed purpose, to overcome inertia, to begin any enterprise, to establish authority, to ensure that commands are obeyed, to obtain a promotion, to get a job that entails rank or authority, to have a presentation or creation accepted. In general for any purpose involving the exercise of willed authority.

The suit of Cups is best used to attract love, to gain a friendship, to ensure a good marriage, to succeed in a social affair, to be accepted into a group, to achieve prophetic dreams or visions, to increase charm and grace, to bewitch, to ensnare the heart of another. In general for any purpose involving empathy or the emotions.

The suit of Swords is useful to discover hidden plans, to penetrate to the heart of a secret or mystery, to expose or confront a foe, to enforce obedience, to punish, to project malicious intentions, to define concepts, to speak or write about intellectual matters, to understand complex details, to win in debates or arguments, to achieve victory in sports or other conflicts. In general for any purpose involving intellectual expression or confrontation.

The suit of Pentacles is used to encourage the growth of plants or crops, to improve health, to engender a child, to make money, to increase possessions, to obtain a place to live, to get work, to foster the growth of an enterprise already established, to be more productive, to cure disease, to become stronger. In general for any purpose involving the body and material increase.

Each of the four elements has attached to it a class of spiritual beings called elementals that are chiefly composed of the lower element to which they belong, and act in the world through the power of that element. The names for these spirits were first used as a set by the German magician and physician Paracelsus (Theophrastus Bombastus von Hohenheim, 1493–1541), who called them salamanders (Fire), undines (Water), sylphs (Air), and gnomes (Earth). These terms were already in existence; Paracelsus merely gathered them under the elements and gave them a more specific meaning.

Elementals may be summoned, instructed, controlled, and banished through the ritual use of their element. An elemental spirit is interacted with during ritual in the same way as a human being, but when dealing with an elemental, the element associated with that spirit must be emphasized so that the ritual circle is saturated with the element and becomes harmonious with the spirit's nature. The way to accomplish this is examined in chapter 26.

Salamanders take their name from the mythical lizard or amphibian fabled to live among the flames and embers of the burning hearth. It was supposed to delight in flame, and to dance through the flames in fireplaces. The spirits of the same name are by nature hot and quick, impetuous, restless, and easily angered or stirred to violent action. They are the least stable of the elementals, and are considered to be the most dangerous and the most difficult to control. Their unseen presence is indicated by a warmth and dryness in the air, or a sense of radiant heat against the surface of the skin, and sometimes by quick flashes of light. Their forms are the least constant of the elemental classes. When visibly manifest, they may be seen as dancing or darting balls of light or flame, or as humanoid figures slender of limb and quick of movement, whose heads at times may be wreathed in flames, or bodies outlined in flickering fire.

The reason salamanders are considered so dangerous is that fires tend to ignite spontaneously where one of these elemental beings is present. This is sometimes attributed to poltergeist activity. When a *poltergeist* (German term for "noisy spirit") focuses its energies obsessively on lighting numerous small fires, it is not unreasonable to refer to that spirit as a Fire elemental. After all, an elemental is merely a spirit that has a predominance of a single element in its nature. Poltergeist activity is often dismissed by those who study it as the physical or psychic manifestations of a disturbed adolescent, but an intelligent spirit of an elemental nature is sometimes involved with the young person, and acts as the agent for the poltergeist activity.

Sylphs are elementals of Air. They usually remain unseen, but when they choose to appear visibly they are more likely to assume human form than salamanders, although their bodies may be translucent. They appear slight and slender, youthful, their fingers long and thin, their necks elongated, their eyes large, their ears large and tending to points, and their faces somewhat triangular. They may be accompanied by vague whisperings, sudden noises, disembodied but distinct voices, sudden winds, breezes, drafts, or coolness. Candle flames will often flutter, curtains or other hanging fabrics will move. A poltergeist of the element Air would be characterized by sudden loud noises or voices, by strong and destructive winds, and by inexplicable drafts and breezes.

It is easier to deal with sylphs than with salamanders, because the Air elementals are more reasoning and intellectual, and so more inclined to respond to human speech, whereas the salamanders are driven by impulses and inarticulate intentions. Sylphs can be employed to acquire information, and to persuade others to adopt a different point of view or opinion.

As we descend to the heavier and denser element Water, it is not surprising to find that the undines are spirits who usually appear in human form, and are less inclined to change their forms capriciously. Their facial features may shift in response to their emotions, which are variable and potent, but their bodies are relatively stable. They appear most often as young and attractive women who are pale of complexion, although male undines also exist. They are passionate and affectionate, extremely loving, and they respond strongly to affection and kindness. Their touch is cool and damp, though not unpleasant. Indeed, they are the most agreeable of the elementals with which to have dealings, both because they are lovely to look upon and because their natures appear superficially to be almost human.

The humanness of their nature is an illusion. Any extended dealings with an undine will quickly show it to be of an unearthly or strange mind. Even though these spirits can talk to human beings and interact with us on a level of friendship or love, they do not see the world as we see it. Their motives are not our motives. The effect is much the same as trying to interact with someone having a mild form of insanity, who appears completely normal most of the time, but who on occasion will act in a way that is unexpected and inexplicable. Fay is a good way to describe the nature of these spirits.

Undines are useful in dealings connected with affection or love, and make good ritual agents in these affairs. A poltergeist associated with elemental Water would be accompanied by showers, rain storms, dampness, coolness, broken water pipes or plumbing fixtures, and the sudden and unexplained presence of wetness or water on the walls, floors, bedding, or clothing.

Linked to elemental Earth are the gnomes, who often pass among human beings unseen. When they show themselves, it is commonly in the form of human beings of short stature with heavy, powerful bodies and mature faces. Those who come in male form may be bearded. They seldom appear without clothing, which is of a heavy and rough kind, suitable for physical work. Their dark eyes are bright with intelligence, their moods capricious and given to mischief, their voices loud and rough, their speech blunt or even coarse.

Historically, gnomes have been the class of elemental most avidly sought out by magicians because they are supposed to know the locations of buried treasures. Dowsing is an activity that may be linked with gnomes, and in this sense the fables that this class of elemental can help in the location of treasures in the Earth are not completely without merit. Gnomes have a liking for practical jokes, and their statements are not to be taken at face value without examination, since of all classes of elementals, gnomes are the most likely to deceive. Poltergeists in harmony with the Earth element express themselves by the movement of physical objects, which can be quite violent, or the appearance of physical objects from thin air, a spirit phenomenon known as an *apport*.

8

THE COURT CARDS

The sixteen court cards are a kind of bridge, symbolically, between the picture cards of the Greater Arcana and the number cards of the Lesser Arcana. They bear characteristics of both groups. Each card bears a unique image, not a mere repetition of the suit symbol as is true of the number cards in the traditional Tarot, and in this sense the court cards resemble the trumps. Yet their images are not as varied as those of the trumps, but are restricted to individual human figures of four types, and these four types are repeated in each suit. Each individual figure is different from the others, yet the difference is not nearly so obvious as the uniqueness of the trumps. The court cards carry the emblem of their suit, which binds them to the suit, but they are not completely defined by that emblem as is true of the number cards.

Because the court cards show individual human figures of various ages, both male and female, it was natural that they be used in Tarot divination to represent human beings. This is their traditional interpretation—a court card in a divination layout signifies a person. It can also have other meanings, but its primary significance is a human being involved in the question with which the divination is concerned. It is natural to extend this function to Tarot magic. By identifying a particular person with one of the court cards, the manipulation of that card during ritual results in the same desired effect on the person it represents. By placing that card in a ritual context, the same circumstances may be created in the life of the individual.

It is important to be able to accurately identify any human being with the most appropriate court card of the Tarot, so that the manipulation of that card has the strongest effect on the individual it represents. In Tarot divination, the link between court cards and human beings is most often based on external features such as eye color, hair color, and complexion. This method was used in the Golden Dawn and is still the standard method of most fortune tellers. However, it is inaccurate, and has been supplanted by a superior method used by Aleister Crowley that involves linking the court cards with different human personality types. These sixteen types will be examined later, but for now we will look at the underlying factors that determine them.

Each court card has two elemental properties that work in combination to define the nature of the card—the background element and the foreground element. The first is the element that comes from the suit to which the court card belongs. For example, all court cards in Wands have as their base or foundation the element of Fire, which is the element of the entire suit of Wands. The background element of the suit serves as a stable foundation against which the foreground element functions. It is much the same as the astrological relationship between the signs of the zodiac and the planets. The planets act against the background of the signs, which color or modify their meanings.

The foreground elements of the court cards are related to the individual card types in each suit, which are the King, Queen, Knight, and Page. Each of the four court cards in a suit has its own independent elemental property that works in combination with the shared suit element. In the court cards, the foreground element that is specific to the card is more active, whereas the background element that is general to the suit is more passive in its working, yet both are lower elements. Do not confuse the dual functioning of the lower elements in the court cards with the higher spiritual expressions of Fire, Air, and Water represented in the trumps.

The foreground elements of the court cards are assigned to the card types based on the letters in Tetragrammaton, the Hebrew name of God with four letters (written in English Yod-Heh-Vau-Heh, or IHVH). That is to say, the foreground elements are linked with the letters of the name, and the letters of the name are linked with the four card types. In this way, across the bridge of the divine name, the foreground elements are linked with the court cards. It is not necessary to fully understand the esoteric use of Tetragrammaton to learn the placement of the elements on the court cards, but you should know that this placement is not arbitrary. The four Hebrew letters of the divine name relate to the court cards of each suit in the following order:

Yod (Fire)–King

Heh (Water)–Queen

Vau (Air)–Knight

Heh (Earth)–Page

> Foreground / Active

As you can see, Tetragrammaton has two letters that are the same, but they are treated differently based on their position in the divine name, and receive different elements. There is a mystery here that repays meditation. The divine name has both three letters, yet at the same time four letters. Keep this in mind when reflecting that the elements are threefold, when considering only the higher spiritual side of the elements represented in the trumps, yet fourfold, when considering the lower earthly expression of the elements represented by the suits.

When the background element of the suit is combined with the foreground element derived from the divine name, each court card obtains a pair of elements. The working of the more active foreground element of the individual card against the more passive background element of the suit gives each card its unique identity, so that the court cards represent sixteen distinct human types. It is usual to write the foreground element first and the background element second, mirroring the titles of the cards themselves.

King of Wands—Fire of Fire (Lightning: violent and quick strike)

Queen of Wands—Water of Fire (Rainbow: transient refracted image)

Knight of Wands—Air of Fire (Sunlight: constant radiant energy)

Page of Wands—Earth of Fire (Smoke: ascending heated particles)

King of Cups—Fire of Water (Fountain: rapid welling forth)
Queen of Cups—Water of Water (Pond: stagnant reflection)
Knight of Cups—Air of Water (Ocean: active decomposition)
Page of Cups—Earth of Water (Ice: frozen forms)

King of Swords—Fire of Air (Wind: swift pressure brought to bear)

Queen of Swords—Water of Air (Vibration: movement through fixed bulk)

Knight of Swords—Air of Air (Cloud: floating shapes)
Page of Swords—Earth of Air (Dust: solid residue)

King of Pentacles—Fire of Earth (Mountain: violent pressure)
Queen of Pentacles—Water of Earth (Field: quiet nurturing)
Knight of Pentacles—Air of Earth (Plain: steady bearer of life)
Page of Pentacles—Earth of Earth (Grove: secret place of growth)

Each of these elemental pairs produces a unique combination that may be exemplified by a specific force or substance in the natural world. Bear in mind that these compound manifestations are only examples. They show the prevailing quality of the pairs of elements in the court cards. For example, the Water of Fire found in the Queen of Wands is well exemplified by the rainbow because a rainbow reflects and refracts the fiery rays of the sun to create an image that is splendid but fleeting and illusory.

Twelve of these sixteen elemental pairs, along with their compound manifestations, appear in a table at the back of Aleister Crowley's *Book of Thoth* (286), where Crowley associates them with the triplicities of the zodiac. They are part of the general Golden Dawn knowledge that Crowley inherited from his membership in the Order. They are not explicitly linked in this table of the triplicities with the court cards, but it is evident that Crowley intended such a link, because he mentions the Princesses (Pages), which are omitted from the elemental pairs in the table. Elsewhere in the same work (23), he lists all sixteen elemental pairs beside the court cards, without describing their compound manifestations.

In the Golden Dawn Tarot, the Pages (called Princesses by the Golden Dawn) have a somewhat different attribution from the other court cards. They are known as the Thrones of the Aces of their suits. Thus, the Page of Swords is the Throne of the Ace of Swords. This difference reflects the distinction between the three higher active elements that occupy zones above the Earth, and the inert and motionless Earth element, which has no active higher zone. The Pages, in their own nature—considered apart from their suits—are of the Earth element. They mark the transition between the court cards and the number cards. After them follow the Aces, which are the roots of the powers of the lower, earthly elements expressed in the ten number cards of each suit.

The three court cards of each suit that are related to the higher spiritual elements Fire, Air, and Water may be conceived to be connected with the three zones of these elements that surround the Earth. They do not rule these zones, which are ruled by the three trumps linked to the Mother letters. At the same time, their affiliation with these zones makes them not entirely earthy in nature, but elevates them above the Earth in their higher aspect. The Pages are not elevated above the Earth, because they have no higher zone. For the practical purposes of Tarot magic, the ten numbered cards of each suit should be thought of as acting strictly in the sphere of Earth to produce manifest or tangible results. It is the four earthy

Pages that link the other twelve court cards related to the spiritual expressions of the elements in zones above the Earth with the forty number cards residing and acting in the sphere of Earth.

It is an easy matter to extend the table of elemental pairs to include the Pages, and to provide examples for them, as I have done. This is useful because it integrates the Pages with the other court cards. However, it should always be borne in mind that in their fundamental nature, the Pages are different from the other court cards. Their active foreground lower element is Earth, which has almost no active energy. It does not initiate. It receives impressions like wet clay, and then hardens to sustain those impressions. When applying this understanding to the human types represented by the court cards in Tarot magic, it may be observed that children are unformed and still in the process of receiving the impressions that will shape their lives and make them into the adults they will become. Young children have always been associated with the Pages.

Elemental Earth can give the appearance of activity and initiative, but the impulse for that activity comes from elsewhere. It is hidden within the darkness of Earth, but not a part of Earth, in the same way that a seed lying in the ground and ready to burst forth with new life is not a part of the soil that surrounds it. Similarly, children often appear to have independent initiative, but they derive their impulses from suggestions implanted in them, or from the examples of others they observe and imitate. By nature, Earth is receptive rather that projective. It supports higher energies, in the same way a throne supports and symbolizes the divinely inspired will of a monarch. It is easy to mistake the symbol for the thing it represents.

Four court cards relate particularly to the letters of Tetragrammaton. They are the court cards that are wholly composed of a single suit element, and in this sense may be thought of as the pure elementals of the suits.

Yod King of Wands (Fire of Fire)

Heh Queen of Cups (Water of Water)

Vau Knight of Swords (Air of Air)

Heh Page of Pentacles (Earth of Earth)

pure elementals

They form a family unit the sexual interaction of which gives rise to what Crowley termed the "formula of Tetragrammaton" (*The Book of Thoth*, 16). It was the Golden Dawn teaching that the court card types were not eternally fixed, but changed from one to another in an unceasing dynamic interaction that is like a dance of life. Mathers represented this dance by the curious names given to the court cards in the Golden Dawn Tarot. The Kings were also called Knights; the Knights were called Kings or Princes. The naming structure of the court cards in the Golden Dawn Tarot is based on the formula of Tetragrammaton. All human types are expressed by the court cards, and human beings do not remain at one age, or in one social position, but evolve and change. The Knight becomes the King. The Page becomes the Queen. The older generation gives way to the newer generation, and the wheel of life revolves.

Neither Crowley nor Mathers makes a special relationship between the four elementally pure court cards and the letters of Tetragrammaton, but such a relationship seems obvious to me. The single element in each of these four cards sets them apart from the other twelve court cards, each of which is composed of two mingled elements.

You do not need to understand the formula of Tetragrammaton to work Tarot magic, but you should know that the four elemental court cards that relate in a special way to the letters of the name act to express the nature of their suits with a clarity and force that is greater than that of the other court cards. There is no conflict in their internal natures. The King of Wands is the purity of Fire and the clear expression of Wands, and so for the Queen of Cups and Water, the Knight of Swords and Air, and the Page of Pentacles and Earth.

THE SIXTEEN SIGNIFICATORS

The pairs of background and foreground lower elements, in conjunction with zodiacal qualities attributed to each of the court cards by the Golden Dawn, define sixteen distinct human types, eight of which are female and eight male. The term *significator* is applied by Tarot diviners in a narrow sense to the court card chosen to represent the *querent* (the person asking the question) during a divination, but in a more general sense, all sixteen court cards may be called significators, since all court cards stand for human beings.

Kings represent older or mature men. Queens stand for mature women. Knights represent younger men or youths. Pages stand for younger women or girls. Children of either sex who have not yet reached puberty are also placed under the four Pages, because in a magical sense they are sexually neutral or undifferentiated. There is a range in ages from King to Page, so that Kings more often are used for older men or men who have achieved a position of authority, Queens are used for all adult women, Knights are used for men who are still striving to establish their place in the world and for teenage males, and Pages are used for teenage girls who have not yet assumed their place in the world, or for small children of either sex.

It should be mentioned that in the Golden Dawn Tarot, a more distinct division was made between the sexes, as the variations in the names of the court cards suggest. Even very young boys might be linked with the Princes (Knights) rather than with the Princesses (Pages). There is a certain ambiguity, because the Golden Dawn still recognized the age differential between the four court cards—the Princesses were understood to be younger than the Princes. This tendency to make an absolute division between the Princes and Princesses based on sex was a departure from the traditional Tarot practice. In traditional divination, young children of either sex are associated with the Pages, and I believe this the better way.

The Golden Dawn also linked human beings to the court cards by hair color and eye color. It was an elaboration of the traditional method used by Tarot fortune tellers for choosing a significator for the querent, and for matching the court cards that turned up in a divination layout with human beings. For example, under the Golden Dawn system, a mature man with fair hair and blue eyes would be given the King of Cups as his significator card; or if the King of Cups appeared in the divination layout, it would be assumed to stand for an older man with blond hair and blue eyes who was involved in the question.

The limitations of this system of assignment are obvious. Not all men with fair hair and blue eyes have the same personality. Some are timid while others are bold. Some are enterprising and others lazy. Some are kind and others malicious. Yet only one human personality type correctly matches the King of Cups. Aleister Crowley completely did away with the assignment of significators by physical indicators. Instead, he relied on personality profiles, and made no mention of hair and eye color in his descriptions of the human types linked to the court cards. Under Crowley's revised method of assignment, a mature man who is easy going, graceful, and sensitive would receive the King of Cups as his significator no matter what he might look like, whether he was a blond Norwegian or a black Moroccan. Crowley did not change the personality types of the court cards from those of the Golden Dawn; he merely omitted the physical indicators linked to the court cards.

In the Golden Dawn system, the King, Queen, and Knight of each suit are each esoterically associated with a thirty-degree arc of the zodiac, and this segment of the zodiac has an important bearing on how the personality types of these twelve court cards are determined. The cards are not assigned a full zodiac sign, as might be supposed. Each court card other than the Pages gets ten degrees from one sign and twenty degrees from an adjacent sign. The sign giving twenty degrees has more influence on the personality type than the sign giving ten degrees, but they are always considered together for their combined influence.

As has already been emphasized, the Pages are treated differently from the other court cards. The Golden Dawn assigned each Page to a full quarter of the heavens around the celestial north pole, along with the corresponding Aces, which were placed nearer to the pole. In this way, the Pages both comprehend a quarter of the zodiac by their arc, yet are separate from it, since the zodiac is confined to a narrow band around the ecliptic, and does not extend to the celestial pole. This assignment of the Pages to the celestial sphere also shows the close relationship in the Golden Dawn system between the Page and the Ace of each suit, and illustrates that the Pages mediate between the Aces and the other court cards. Although the Aces are not shown on the accompanying diagram of the celestial northern hemisphere, they should be understood to occupy the very center of the diagram, in the angles created by the Pages of their suits.

Strictly speaking, the thirty-degree arc of each of the court cards other than the Pages would start with the 21° of the first sign and extend to the 20° of the second sign it occupies, but below I have given the locations of the cards as they are given in Regardie's *Golden Dawn*, which was probably the way the placements of the court cards were described in the original Golden Dawn document *Book T*, which Regardie reproduces. The significant fact to grasp is that one-third of the first sign bears on the card, and two-thirds of the second sign. Similarly, each Page really extends from the 6° of the first sign it covers to the 5° of the last sign, but I have retained Regardie's rounded degree designations.

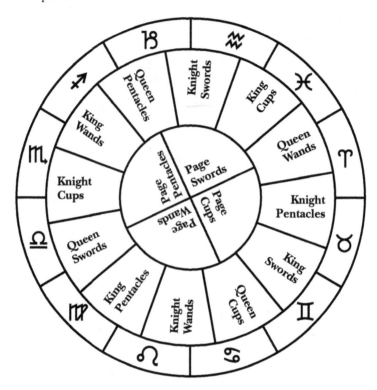

Zodiacal Correspondences of the Court Cards

Each court card describes a different human personality type that is based on the suit of that card, its pair of elements, and the unequal interaction of its two zodiac signs. Since each personality has both a good and a bad side, depending on the factors that influence its development and the circumstances that affect it at any given moment, there are two descriptions for each card—its personality type at its best, and that same personality type when at its worst.

King of Wands—Fire of Fire (20° Scorpio to 20° Sagittarius)
An older man, or a mature man in an established position, who is impulsive, impetuous, prideful, swift to take action, unpredictable, and lacking in endurance. His worst qualities are a tendency to cruelty and intolerance.

Queen of Wands—Water of Fire (20° Pisces to 20° Aries)
A mature woman of calm authority who is adaptable and persistent, generous, and loving, but sometimes impatient of contradiction. Her worst qualities are a tendency to be obstinate and vengeful toward those who defy her.

Knight of Wands—Air of Fire (20° Cancer to 20° Leo)
A younger man or youth of an honorable and generous nature, fond of practical jokes, romantic, opinionated, and argumentative, who sometimes acts without thinking. His worst qualities are a tendency to be boastful and to avoid hard work, and indifference to the suffering of others.

Page of Wands—Earth of Fire (5° Cancer to 5° Libra)
A young woman or girl who is full of enthusiasm and energy, who is daring, reckless, forceful. Her worst qualities are a tendency to be overly dramatic, shallow, unfeeling toward others, unreliable, and overbearing.

King of Cups—Fire of Water (20° Aquarius to 20° Pisces)
An older man, or a mature man in an established position, who is graceful, easy-going, sensitive, and easily roused to enthusiasm but with no enduring passions. His worst qualities are a tendency to untruthfulness, passive indifference, sensual indulgence, and weakness of character.

Queen of Cups—Water of Water (20° Gemini to 20° Cancer)
A mature woman of patient, languid, dreaming disposition, tranquil in manner, who responds like a mirror to the emotions that surround her. Her worst qualities are a tendency to be easily led astray by bad advice and bad company.

Knight of Cups—Air of Water (20° Libra to 20° Scorpio)
A younger man or youth of a secretive and subtle nature, who is artistic, outwardly placid but inwardly passionate, and ruthless in pursuit of his ends. His worst qualities are a tendency to be irresponsible,

indifferent toward others, lacking in conscience, crafty, and apt to use concealed violence.

Page of Cups—Earth of Water (5° Aries to 5° Cancer)
A young woman or girl who is gentle, kind, tender hearted, and a friend in need who can be relied on. Her worst qualities are a tendency to be dreamy and self-absorbed, and to be overly dependent on others.

King of Swords—Fire of Air (20° Taurus to 20° Gemini)
A older man, or a mature man in an established position, who is active, clever, skillful, sometimes inspired, courageous, and enthusiastic. His worst qualities are a tendency to expend his energies in futile efforts, and to become indecisive and purposeless.

Queen of Swords—Water of Air (20° Virgo to 20° Libra)
A mature woman of independent nature, who is confident in herself, honorable, fair, keenly observant, physically graceful, fond of dancing, and a reliable witness. Her worst qualities are a tendency to be sly and unreliable, unfeeling toward others, and to use her charms to deceive.

Knight of Swords—Air of Air (20° Capricorn to 20° Aquarius)
A younger man or youth who is idealistic, intellectual, full of plans and purposes, clever, and rational, but unstable. His worst qualities are a tendency to adopt fads or join movements without any real conviction, to debate or contest the status quo merely for the sake of debate.

Page of Swords—Earth of Air (5° Capricorn to 5° Aries)
A younger woman or girl who is practical, firm, determined, somewhat stern in her manner, and skillful in handling material affairs. Her worst qualities are a tendency to become unfocused in her purpose or underhanded when overwhelmed by practical difficulties.

King of Pentacles—Fire of Earth (20° Leo to 20° Virgo)
An older man, or a mature man in an established position, who is dull, ponderous, and slow to act, but is also a hard worker possessing limitless patience and determination in the material sphere. His worst qualities are a tendency to become sullen, surly, resentful of achievement in others, and petty-minded.

Queen of Pentacles—Water of Earth (20° Sagittarius to 20° Capricorn)
A mature woman who is affectionate, large hearted, intuitive, sensible, and down to earth, with a practical approach to life. Her worst qualities are a tendency to become addicted to drugs, alcohol, or sex, and to be servile and foolish.

Knight of Pentacles—Air of Earth (20° Aries to 20° Taurus)
A younger man or youth who is competent, reliable, enduring, thoughtful, not easily provoked, adaptable, cautious, and a maker of plans. His worst qualities are a tendency to be emotionless, insensitive, uninterested in things outside his own sphere, and resentful of what he considers airy-fairy nonsense.

Page of Pentacles—Earth of Earth (5° Libra to 5° Capricorn)
A younger woman or girl who is strong, poised, inwardly quiet, patient, material, nurturing, brave, and capable of deep loyalty and affections. Her worst qualities are a tendency to become unstable, wasteful, and to do things to excess and squander her resources.

10

THE TEN SEPHIROTH

The number cards in the suits of the Lesser Arcana are linked in their higher aspects with the ten Sephiroth, stages in the process of the dynamic and ceaseless emanation of the universe from the primal source to the material world. Although the number cards act in the lower world of the four elements to realize the practical results of Tarot magic, it is necessary to take into consideration their higher, more spiritual associations to fully understand them.

The Sephiroth are part of the system of Jewish mysticism and magic known as the Kabbalah, and they figure prominently in its oldest and most authoritative text, *Sepher Yetzirah*, upon which the Tarot correspondences of the Golden Dawn are based. The Sephiroth are not merely the simple numbers from one to ten, but are the living, intelligent spirits of the numbers that sustain and empower them, each equivalent to a primary name of God, for according to the Kabbalah the stages in the emanation of the universe are not separate from the creator, but ever remain connected to the body of God.

The distinction between the Sephiroth and the numbers is stressed in *Sepher Yetzirah*, where in the first chapter it is written, "The ineffable Sephiroth are Ten, as are the Numbers," and a little further on in the same chapter, "The ineffable Sephiroth give forth the Ten numbers" (Westcott, *Sepher Yetzirah*, 15–16). It is in this sense that the Sephiroth are the higher aspects of the numbers, and of the number cards of the suits. The numbers are manifest expressions *restriction*

S
E
V (F)
E
R
I
T
Y

M
I
D
D
L
E

M
E
R
C
Y (M)

—Initiative   spiritual (1)

Material (10)

of the Sephiroth, and should not be mistaken for the Sephiroth themselves.

In Western magic, the Sephiroth are usually shown as circles that are intended to represent spheres arranged on a symbolic design generally known as the Tree of Life, which was of key importance in the Golden Dawn system of magic. The Tree of Life has had numerous forms over the course of its evolution, but the pattern adopted by the Golden Dawn is that of Athanasius Kircher (1601–80), illustrated in his 1652 work *Oedipus Aegyptiacus* (Seligmann, *The History of Magic*, 355). The Golden Dawn Tree does not reproduce the Tree of Kircher in all its minor details, but the overall structure is the same. It is composed of three columns. The central column is balanced in its properties and is called the Middle Pillar. The right column is the Pillar of Mercy, and it is of a masculine, expansive nature. The left column is the Pillar of Severity, and has a feminine, restrictive nature. There are four Sephiroth on the Middle Pillar, three on the Pillar of Mercy, and three on the Pillar of Severity.

Creative energy descends down the Tree in a zigzag path, reflecting from one side of the Tree to the other in a progress that is known as the Way of the Lightning, because it resembles a lightning bolt falling from the heavens to the earth. It follows the numbers of the Sephiroth, beginning with one and ending with ten. There is a reflux of this energy that rises up from the earth and ascends to heaven once again, but it is not as direct as the Way of the Lightning. It touches all twenty-two channels or paths that link the spheres of the Sephiroth together in the course of its ascent, and for this reason is known as the Way of the Serpent.

In general, it may be said that the Sephiroth on the Right Pillar of the Tree initiate and project forth their energies, seeking unrestricted realization of their natures. Unchecked, this wildly expanding force would be destructive. It is kept under restraint and limited by the Sephiroth on the Left Pillar of the Tree, which set the bounds upon its action. It is not that one side is good and the other evil, as is sometimes mistakenly assumed. It would be better to characterize the right side of the Tree as inspired enthusiasm, and the left side as sober analysis. The Middle Pillar both provides the essence that empowers all the Sephiroth, and balances its distribution on the Tree so that it does not fly apart and destroy itself.

The four Aces are associated with the highest sphere, Kether, through the number one, and in their spiritual aspects lie outside the process by which the universe was emanated. Kether is the godhead, the source of creation within which and from which all forms and energies are differentiated, but it has no form and no energy of itself. It is for this reason that the Aces are called the roots of the powers of the elements. The Aces are pure elemental potential, and from their source the differentiated elemental qualities of the rest of the cards of the Minor Arcana take their origin.

The four Tens are linked with the lowest sphere, Malkuth, the end of creation in which all that went before finds realization. It is the Sephirah that represents the sphere of the material world, and is known in the Kabbalah as the *Aulam Yesodoth,* the sphere of the elements, because in Malkuth the elements find their densest material expression.

Between the spiritualized elements of Kether at the top of the Tree, and the materialized elements of Malkuth at the bottom, lie the Sephiroth of the heavenly spheres—the seven spheres of the planets, and the eighth sphere of the fixed stars or zodiac, against the backdrop of which the planets wander.

In the system of magic used by the Golden Dawn, the number cards from Two to Ten derive much of their meaning from their location on the Tree. Part of the meaning stems from the name of each Sephirah, part from its placement on the Tree, and part from the heavenly sphere associated with that Sephirah. A study of the Tree of Life will greatly aid in the accurate application of the number cards in Tarot magic. Only by understanding the higher meaning of the number cards can they be successfully used in their lower manifest expression to define the ritual purpose.

Comprehensive understanding of the entire structure of the Tree requires months of study and meditation. There is no need at present to examine its deeper mysteries. What we are concerned with

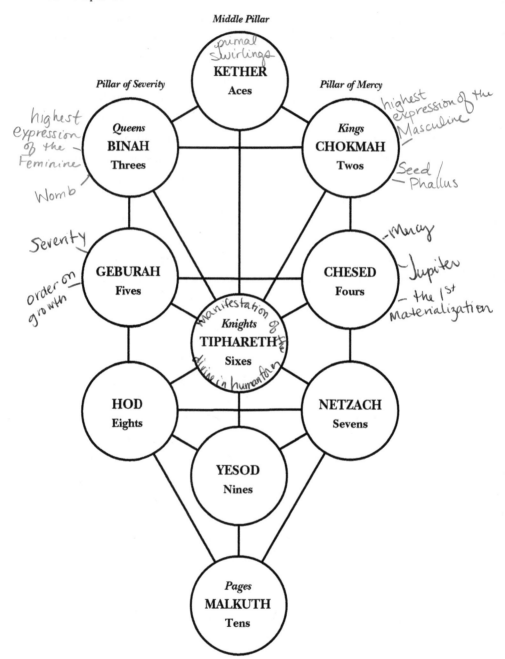

Suit Cards on the Tree of Life

in this book is the way in which the Sephiroth influence the identities of the number cards of the suits in the Golden Dawn system. By learning the meanings of the Sephiroth, we can better grasp the meanings of the number cards.

Aces—Kether (the Crown)—Primal Swirlings

Twos—Chokmah (Wisdom)—Zodiac

Threes—Binah (Understanding)—Saturn

Fours—Chesed (Mercy)—Jupiter

Fives—Geburah (Severity)—Mars

Sixes—Tiphareth (Beauty)—Sun

Sevens—Netzach (Victory)—Venus

Eights—Hod (Glory)—Mercury

Nines—Yesod (the Foundation)—Moon

Ten—Malkuth (the Kingdom)—Four elements

Kether is the Crown of Creation, the unknowable source from Source Energy which all things proceed. Creation is conceived in the Kabbalah not to be a flowing out from Kether, but rather a primal swirling of the substance of Kether into a vortex that gives all created things their initial identity or being. Identity arises from variations in the density of the otherwise uniform and undifferentiated essence of the source. The other nine Sephiroth exist inside of Kether, as does the entire manifest universe, since all is composed of Kether.

It is in this sense that the Aces are known as the roots of the elements. From the Aces proceed all the number cards of the suits. Their action is powerful, primal, expansive, like the flowing forth of a fountain. What is perceived in Kether as a swirling into the center is perceived in the world as a fountaining outward. In ALTAR Tarot magic, the Aces are used as the ritual instruments of the four elements and together constitute the altar.

Chokmah, or Wisdom, is the primordial Father, also known as Abba, the highest expression of the masculine principle—seminal, potent, willful, projective. To it is assigned the sphere of the fixed stars, or zodiac. It may be thought of as the phallus of God. Its nature is like a seed, tiny and hard, its creative fire concealed within its center.

The Twos partake of the force of the primordial ray expressed by Chokmah, the first emanation from Kether. In two there is reciprocation, duality, and the potential for conflict although no conflict has yet arisen.

Binah, or Understanding, is the primordial Mother, also known as Aima, the highest expression of the feminine principle—fertile, receptive, formative, nurturing. To it is assigned the sphere of Saturn. It may be thought of as the womb of God. Its nature resembles the sea, vast and salty like the blood that nourishes new life, and teaming in its shadowed depths with countless forms.

The Threes express the creative energy of the womb of Binah. They fulfill the third point of the highest triangle of the Sephiroth and in this way show balance and reconciliation.

Chesed, or Mercy, is the first emanation below the perfect trine of the Supernals—the highest three Sephiroth. It is the first materialization, and as such, the highest concept that can be directly examined by the mind. The formless inspirations of Chokmah, given ideal patterns within the womb of Binah, issue forth in Chesed. To it is assigned Jupiter.

The Fours embody the solidification of the ideal, the making manifest of the unformed or concealed. They begin the second trine on the Tree.

Geburah, or Severity, on the left side of the Tree is a reaction to Chokmah on the right side. Whereas Chokmah expands forth into manifestation, Geburah restricts that expansion so that it does not run riot and dissolve into chaos. It is the imposition of order on growth by the process of pruning or cutting back. To it is assigned Mars.

The Fives are the limiting or restricting of enthusiasm for the preservation of order. When this restriction is carried too far, it be-

comes burdensome and is looked upon as a punishment or afflic-
tion, but it is not in itself evil.

Tiphareth, or Beauty, on the Middle Pillar of the Tree is its
center, and the seat of the Messiah or Christos (Anointed One)—
the manifestation of divine energy in human form. It is a reflection of Kether above it, and completes the second trine on the
Tree. To it is given the perfect and unchanging Sun in the Golden
Dawn system.

The Sixes are the radiant light of consciousness in its most harmonious and balanced expression—what is called higher consciousness. At this stage all four elements reach their perfect evolution,
without as yet any excess or decay.

Netzach, or Victory, on the right side of the Tree expresses the
unbalanced expansive use of the force in Tiphareth, resulting in
illusion and disappointment. That which was perfect is made to
serve imperfect ends, and is distorted as a result. To it is given
the planet Venus.

The Sevens express degeneration and excess, the misuse of the
higher for the lower. Imbalance causes weakness amid an abundance of force, as strength works against itself. The victory is hol-
low. Emotional creation without critical judgment produces wild
frenzies of passion that lack maturity.

Hod, or Glory, on the left of the Tree balances Netzach in the
third trine of emanation. Like Geburah above it, a reaction oc-
curs to the expansive action of its opposite sphere on the far side
of the Tree. Hod channels the creative excess of Netzach into intellectual forms of expression that become too studied, too med-
dling and inhibiting. To it is linked the planet Mercury.

The Eights are an excess of expression that appears lifeless because all passion has been redirected into trivial, sterile channels.
Everything is over-examined and talked to death. Experience is
not immediate and free, but stylized and composed.

Yesod, or the Foundation, on the Middle Pillar completes the
third trine of the Sephiroth. Imbalance of effort is stabilized in

the final stage of emanation before the bringing forth of the material universe. The light of consciousness from Tiphareth directly above is thickened and given persistent shape, like cooling wax poured into a mold. To it is assigned the Moon, the gatekeeper of the heavens.

The Nines are the crystallization of the elemental energies flowing through the suits, the final stage of their evolution before they become fixed in matter. There is strong duality in all of them, like the dark and bright faces of the Moon, since this formative energy can be well or ill used, but in either instance is potent in its density.

Malkuth, or the Kingdom, at the base of the Tree is not a part of the three trines above, but stands alone. There is no energy of mutation or evolution here. The elements have reached their fulfillment. They are dense, opaque, burdensome, but at the same time solid and enduring. There is no planet here, only the interaction of the four lower elements.

The Tens bear the entire process of creation within themselves. They show the natural consequence of carrying the elemental potencies down to the physical world. There is no reaction to their expressions. They are inert. Yet reaction is implied since nothing can endure forever, and existence is change.

11

SYMBOLIC TOOLS
OF TAROT MAGIC

In traditional Western ceremonial magic, or the more modern systems of magic based on it such as that taught by the Golden Dawn, various instruments are used during rituals in order to bring about willed purposes. Most of these tools are physical objects. Among the more important tools are the wand, the sword, the lamp, the knife, the altar, the ring, the cup, the sash, the robe, the lamen, the temple or ritual chamber, the pillars, and the banners of the quarters; there are many others that vary from system to system. They are often beautiful and precious objects, expensive and difficult to make. This alone has inhibited many individuals who might otherwise have pursued the study of ceremonial magic. They fear they do not possess the skill to make the instruments correctly, they cannot afford to buy them already made, or they do not have a room in their house that they can set aside as a temple wholly for ritual work.

However, the effectiveness of ritual instruments does not depend on the substances from which they are made, or how lavishly they are decorated. It is not even a function of the rituals that accompany their making and consecration, or the names and sigils of power that may be inscribed on them. It is inherent in their very forms. The details of their construction are at best aids to the working of these instruments, or at worst mere ornamentation.

Tarot magic uses a simplified set of symbolic tools that are created by the placement and relationship of the cards laid out in a

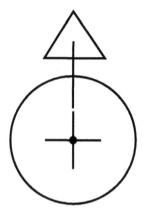

Symbolic Tools

ritual. The basic tools are the point, the ray, the circle, the triangle, and the cross. The accompanying schematic diagram shows the typical arrangement of these tools during rituals. In the following chapters we will examine each tool in detail, describing the cards used in its creation and how they are arranged, but here I wish to consider them symbolically, as shapes, in relation to one another.

THE POINT

Tarot magic uses single cards as points of focus. They act as vessels to hold the light of consciousness of the magician as it shifts from card to card during the ritual, and by their nature define where and how the force of the will is projected to accomplish the ritual purpose. Consciousness can only occupy a single point at any moment, and the mind can only hold a single thought at any one time. By changing the awareness from one card to another, a movement and direction is given to the will. The most important single card is the significator of the magician, which occupies the altar at the center of the ritual circle. It is home for the point of view and self-identity of the magician, as well as the symbolic center of the universe during the ritual.

Wherever the awareness resides becomes the center of the universe. All mathematical points are the same, because all are featureless and without dimension. For this reason, they are interchangeable. Any point of focus for consciousness anywhere in the universe becomes the center of the universe for that consciousness when the point is occupied. Any single card may serve as a temporary point of focus. In a symbolic sense, a single card is equivalent to a point. The point is located or designated in a physical way during ritual by touching the card with the index finger.

All points are also gateways that may be looked through or passed through. To do this, they must be opened, and the symbolic mechanism that opens any point into a gateway is the spiral or vortex. A card may be thought of as an already opened gateway that gives access to a world or symbolic landscape defined by the nature of the design on the card. The design is a kind of window on that world, but it is also possible to step through that opening into the world of the card and experience its balance of forces.

THE RAY

The ray is a straight line that defines the shift of the awareness from one point to another. Any two points define a ray, when considered with the mind one after the other. Strictly speaking, there is no movement between points, only one point in the awareness, followed by a different point. Due to the way the mind works, the illusion of movement is created, in the same way that still images played one after another through a cinema film projector will created the illusion of continuous motion on a screen.

Awareness can carry power with it through the focused application of the will. Force projected along a ray may either be projected in one direction like an arrow fired from a bow, or it may have a reciprocal pulse, so that the ray connects the two points interactively. These are known in my own system of magic as reciprocating rays. By occupying one point with the awareness, and sustaining a reciprocating ray that links with another point, a reflux is achieved between the points. Consciousness dances along the ray from point to point, and back again, so that it seems to occupy two points simultaneously—something that is not really possible, yet through the use of a reciprocating ray appears possible.

In Tarot magic, a ray is projected using two single cards that represent its beginning and end points. Any two Tarot cards can be used to project a ray, although the starting point is usually the significator of the magician. The first card tapped by the index finger marks the origin of the ray, and the second card touched by the same finger defines both its direction and its focus. When the ray is reciprocal, the first card is tapped again to indicate the returning pulse, and a union is created between the things represented by the two cards. This may be sustained for as long as the two cards are not moved from their places.

THE CIRCLE

The circle is one of the earliest and most indispensable tools of ritual magic. Its purpose is to create a smaller, separate universe that is divided from the greater universe. The space within the magic circle is symbolically cut off from the rest of the world by the continuous, unbroken line of the circle. Do not think of this so much as a physical division or barrier, but conceive it as one complete concept that is separate and distinct from another complete concept. By dividing the inner working space from the outer world, the interior of the circle is protected from intrusions, distractions, and contaminations of an astral kind, since on the astral level, symbols are real and tangible barriers.

The circle can also be charged with whatever occult energy is most conducive to the fulfillment of the ritual purpose. When charged, it may be used like a capacitor to release all its energy in a single moment along a ray of will. This is the practice of Wiccan covens, which raise occult force within the ritual circle by means of dancing, chants, and a collective will that is focused on the high priestess of the coven. This sort of energy accumulation, which automatically assumes a spiral form, is known as a cone of power. At the height of the ritual, the high priestess releases the accumulated energy along a ray to fulfill whatever purpose the ritual was designed to accomplish.

In the traditional Western ceremonial magic described in the grimoires, the emphasis is on the circle as a barrier of protection. Magicians often evoked spirits of an infernal or chthonic nature, and relied on the circle to remain safe from the beings they called forth into tangible perception. In modern Wicca, the circle is usually understood to be a way of accumulating and holding ritual energy. Its protective properties have been largely forgotten. You should understand that the circle serves both these functions, and both are important.

The ritual circle used in Tarot magic is formed with the twelve trumps of the zodiac, which are laid out on the table or other working surface in a ring that is a mirror reflection of the zodiacal circle of the heavens, beginning at the east with Aries and proceeding in the usual sequence of the signs clockwise, instead of counterclockwise.

THE TRIANGLE

Traditional evocation is done through the instrument of a ritual triangle inscribed outside the boundary of the circle, and pointing away from the circle. In a symbolic sense, spirits or spiritual energies are evoked, or called forth, within the triangle by expanding the point at its apex down to its base with a vortex, thereby opening a portal in the point of the apex and drawing whatever is evoked into the triangle, where it is sustained.

A distinction must be made between evocation and invocation because these two practices are so often confused. Evocation involves a "calling out" whereas invocation is a "calling in." Magicians used evocation to call forth spirits to perceptible appearance outside the boundary of the protective magic circle. The triangle was used to focus the evocation and make it more effective. It was not a prison for the evoked spirit or a barrier, but more of a stage upon which the spirit made its appearance. The spirit usually remained in the triangle because the triangle was shaped with words and symbols agreeable to that spirit, and inscribed with words of power having authority over the spirit. Often the triangle also contained substances in harmony with the nature of the spirit.

Evocation was used for dangerous or malicious spirits, as a way for the magician to question them or give them commands while at the same time remaining separate and secure from them. Invocation was used for friendly spirits as a way of calling them into a magic circle, or into a particular space or environment, or even summoning them into the body of the magician so that the magician could assume their power and authority temporarily.

The triangle is seldom used in modern magic because very little ritual evocation is done by modern magicians. However, as a general symbolic tool of manifestation, it is unparalleled. No ritual structure is better suited for actualizing or making real something that as yet exists only in a potential way, such as an idea or a plan. The triangle can be used to call forth into being much more than spirits. By its inherent shape, it can be used to assist in the realization of the ritual purpose.

The triangle is defined in Tarot magic by the three trumps of the higher, active elements: the Fool (Air), the Hanged Man (Water), and Judgement (Fire). The bases of the cards are interwoven so that their sides tilt up slightly and define a rotating vortex. This tilt is more pronounced with smaller cards. The Fool is set at the apex of the triangle, and acts as the portal of entry into the triangle, with the Hanged Man at its base on the left and Judgement at its base on the right. The zero that has since the time of Court de Gébelin been associated with the Fool represents very well the mathematical point opened into a doorway by a spiral vortex. This same opened point is expressed physically by the tiny triangular gap where the bases of the three trumps meet and overlap.

THE CROSS

In Golden Dawn magic, the square top of the altar embodies in its shape the four lower elements. The altar defines the practical working surface of the ritual. It represents in miniature the innermost fixed realm of the Earth in the Ptolemaic model of the universe, just as the magic circle represents the all-encompassing outermost sphere that marks its boundary. The active instruments of the elements used by the Golden Dawn—the Rod, the Cup, the Dagger, and the Pentacle—are physical objects patterned after the four suit symbols of the Tarot, and are used to manipulate the energies of the elements. During ritual these instruments are laid out on the surface of the altar so that they rest on the points of an imaginary cross that has as its center the altar flame.

It is natural to equate the four Aces with the four ritual instruments of the elements. Each Ace usually bears a single large symbol of its suit, and the elemental instruments are shaped after the suit symbols. The Aces are linked with Kether, the source of creation, and during Golden Dawn rituals the elemental instruments are placed around the lamp at the center of the altar, which symbolically represents the light of Kether. The Aces are the roots of the powers of the elements, flowing forth from the center of being, so each is well suited to embody in a single card the element of its suit.

In Tarot magic, the altar is composed of the four Aces laid out in a cross pattern. The bases of the four cards are interlaced in such a way that they are tilted and with their raised side edges define a turning vortex. This tilt is much more noticeable with smaller cards. Where their bases join is a tiny square hole representing the central point of the altar, which is occupied by the awareness of the magician during rituals. This central space between the cards takes the place of the altar lamp.

12

THE POINT

At any moment during a ritual of Tarot magic, the awareness will be focused on only a single card. It is impossible to fix the mind on two cards simultaneously because only one thing can be held in the mind at one time. The mind can focus on the entire circle of zodiacal trumps as a circle, but not as individual cards. It can focus on the Aces of the altar as a cross, but not on more than one individual Ace. Consequently, the activity of ritual involves shifting the awareness from one card to another, and holding the cards in the mind successively. The mind may jump very rapidly from card to card, so that they are blended together in the same way that the letters of a word blend when it is spoken, but at any given instant it will be fixed on no more than a single card.

In Tarot divination, as has already been mentioned, a single court card that represents the person seeking the reading is known as the significator. It stands for that person in the layout of the cards. The significator is a bit of traditional lore that has been carried forward from older French methods of fortune telling such as those used by Etteilla, an early exponent of the Tarot, as an instrument of divination. Many modern forms of divination do not use a significator, nor is it needed to tell fortunes with the cards. However, in Tarot magic, significators are essential.

The sixteen court cards are the significators of Tarot magic. Any of them may represent a human being involved in the ritual. Most important among them is the card selected to stand for the person performing the ritual. It is placed face up on the altar, at the center of the ritual circle formed by the twelve trumps of the zodiac. It is by using a significator to represent the magician that Tarot magic can be worked on the surface of a small table. Were it necessary for the magician to physically stand inside the ritual circle, the circle would have to be made much larger and placed on the floor. It is a great virtue of Tarot magic that its entire apparatus can be carried in the pocket, and laid out on a tabletop.

During rituals the magician projects his or her identity and point of view into the center of the circle, just as though physically standing within it. The significator card becomes the vessel that contains the magician's identity.

The court cards are intermediaries that connect the trumps representing higher celestial forces with the number cards representing material motives and events in the physical world. In the same way, the magician who stands at the center of the ritual structure manipulates and applies the higher forces of the trumps to accomplish the mundane purposes represented by the number cards. This central place of the magician is suggested by the location of Tiphareth, the central sixth Sephirah on the Tree of Life that is the seat of the Christos or Messiah. The Anointed One of religious myth is a human being who has been infused with divine wisdom and power from Kether, and who expresses that divinity in a manifest way in the lower world of the four elements in Malkuth. He stands with his feet on the ground and his head in the heavens, uniting the highest with the lowest.

Your significator must always be chosen from among the court cards, and should be the card that most closely expresses your nature. It should be the court card in harmony with your personality, and need not reflect your physical appearance, although older men should usually choose a significator from the Kings and mature women a significator from among the Queens, whereas younger men should choose one of the Knights and younger women one of the Pages. Always use the same court card for your significator. Set it upright, from your own perspective, in the center of the circle.

Regardless of the orientation of the other cards, the significator is always placed upright from your point of view. It represents you. During ritual, mentally project yourself into that card, and imagine that you are standing within the circle of zodiacal trumps. As much as possible you must strive to become the significator card.

During Tarot magic all of the cards lie flat, or nearly so. Each card has a three-dimensional astral projection, and these are visualized as upright rectangles of light that float in the air above the cards that lie beneath them. For practical purposes, during rituals it is best to imagine yourself standing upright upon an enlarged version of the significator card, rather than trying to become the human figure illustrated on the surface of the card, or looking out through the figure's eyes. Think of the card as a kind of rug that lies flat on the floor of the astral place of working, decorated with the image of the court figure, and imagine that you stand upright on the rug.

When performing a ritual that has as its focus another human being, a second significator is chosen to represent that person from among the fifteen remaining court cards. Where this second significator is placed will depend on the type of magic being worked. Most frequently it should be put at the center of the triangle outside the zodiacal circle, since the triangle is used to realize the ritual purpose.

The focus of a ritual is not always a person, but may be an event, a place, an object, a business, a contract, an action, or something else, and in this case the card placed on the triangle will not be drawn from the court cards, but from the number cards of the Minor Arcana. A number card is selected that best represents the intention of the ritual realized.

By using more than one card in the triangle to express the fulfillment of the ritual purpose, it is possible to define and direct the fulfillment in desired ways, but no more than three number cards should be used, in addition to a significator, within the triangle. As more and more number cards are combined to express the purpose, that expression becomes less clear, until eventually with enough cards a point is reached when it collapses into chaos. Three cards of realization are about the maximum that can be used effectively. It is impossible to hold three cards in the mind at once, but they can be considered successively, as a series of actions leading to the final achievement of the ritual purpose.

During acts of magic in which the magician represents another individual, and works the magic on the other person's behalf, becoming in effect the agent for that person, the significator chosen to represent the person should be placed under the significator of the magician in the center of the circle. This is done to symbolically unite the two into one.

Two court significators may be overlaid within the circle for other reasons. For example, if the magician wishes to psychically communicate with another person, joining the significators within the circle is a workable method. Thoughts or images are easily projected from the magician to the other individual in this way, and the thoughts or emotions of the other person will find their way into the mind of the magician. This technique can be a good way for getting to know another person on a deep level. It is best used only with someone who is loved and trusted, since he or she is invited into the circle with the magician. When two court cards are overlaid on the altar, the identities of the magician and the other person who is the focus of the ritual become merged.

The significator of the magician should always be placed on top of any other card or cards on the altar. This is the dominant position. It should always be upright from the magician's viewpoint, never upside down. This is true even when the significator of the magician is alone at the center of the circle. Reversal of the significator will hinder the magician in the free expression of his or her will.

For all other cards, the upright position is defined by the center of the circle, or in the special case of the three elemental trumps, by the center of the triangle. Cards are considered to be upright when they have their bases toward the center of the circle, or in the case of the three elemental trumps that form the triangle, when they have their bases toward the center of the triangle. The significator of the magician, and any other significator that may lie directly beneath it on the central altar, are oriented as upright from the perspective of the magician. Significators or number cards on the triangle are orientated with their bases toward the center of the circle.

EXERCISE OF THE POINT

The transference of your point of view from your own body into your significator requires practice but is essential. The viewpoint is the place you imagine your awareness to occupy. Usually, we tend to assume that our perspective on the world is our physical brain, and that we look outward from our skull through our eyes upon the rest of the world. This is only a conventional belief, and a magician is not bound by it. The entire perceived universe is created within your own mind, and resides within your mind. It is vital to understand and accept this truth. You do not exist in the world; the world exists within you. Because of this, you have the power to shift your point of awareness into anything you perceive.

Whatever may or may not exist completely outside of your own mind, if indeed the human mind can be said to have a boundary, is beyond your ability to perceive or interact with, or even to imagine, in any way whatsoever. For you, it does not exist. What exists and has reality for you lies within your mind, and only within your mind, and this is why you, as a magician, have power over it. Since everything is a part of your mind, you have power over everything. You are shackled by the conventional teachings absorbed in your childhood, the limited perspective of science, the modern cult of materialism, all of which try to tell you that you cannot control the so-called outer world that lies beyond your body. This is a lie. Both your body and the world exist in your own mind, as part of your mind.

The ability to manipulate and control the point of view is in large measure a function of how you understand your reality. If you remain convinced that there is an absolute boundary between inside your body and outside your body, you will find it difficult to effectively project your consciousness into material objects, or to occupy with awareness your astral form and change its shape, or its location in space. On the other hand, if you realize and accept that both your body and the external environment in which it functions are constructs of your own mind, it will be easier to learn the trick of projecting your point of view beyond your skin.

You can practice this technique with the significator you have selected to represent you during rituals lying flat on the table in front of you. Do not stand it on its end. It will lie flat in all rituals of Tarot magic, so you should get used to projecting into it this way. It should be face up, and upright from your point of view. Sit comfortably in your chair, but keep your back upright. Do not slouch since this will inhibit your breathing and the flow of vitality through your body. Look down at the significator card. Briefly examine its overall image to refresh the details in your mind, then focus your eyes on the face of the human figure in the image.

Imagine yourself standing on an enlarged version of the card that lies flat on the black floor of a vast, featureless room. The black floor extends into shadow on all sides so that you cannot see the walls of whatever great chamber you occupy. The ceiling is similarly unseen above you—when you look up there are only shadows. You should get accustomed to creating this featureless space with its black floor, since it will be your typical astral place of working for Tarot rituals.

The court card lies under your feet as though the card were a rug decorated with the court image. The figure is still visible on the card. Feel yourself to be a projection of that figure. All the cards in the astral space have projections that stand upright above them, and you are the projection of your significator. You are both yourself and the noble person depicted on the court card. While performing this exercise, forget as much as possible the existence of your actual body. Imagine that you are looking outward from where you stand on the rug of your significator.

It is better not to imagine that you have shrunk to the size of the card. Rather, imagine that the card has expanded to your own height, and exists on the astral plane in the working space of your rituals, where you project your identity when you visualize yourself standing upon it. The card on the table is only a miniature physical model of this astral reality. Turn around on the axis of your astral body and look about at the astral space, which at present is featureless since the only thing in it is your enlarged significator card and your projected form. During rituals, the astral forms of the other cards will be visible. The black floor is a kind of stage upon which you can enact any ritual drama.

When you are successful in this exercise, you will find that your mind becomes divided. Part of it is still looking down at the significator on the table, but another part is looking outward at the blackness of the ritual space while standing on the enlarged astral version of the card. Your point of view will shift back and forth from one place to the other. You will need to keep renewing the astral space in your imagination in order to remain present within it. This gets easier with practice. The best form of practice is to actually work rituals, but in the beginning it is useful to spend some time projecting your awareness into the significator alone.

Do not expect that you will at once be able to project yourself so completely and perfectly into the card that you forget your physical body. At some point you may achieve this level of ability, but Tarot magic can be worked with only a partial projection of the awareness into the card. If you can achieve the divided state of consciousness in which you are simultaneously in your body, yet standing within the astral space on the rug of the significator, you will be able to perform successful rituals.

13

THE RAY

A dynamic relationship exists between your significator and any other card that forms a part of the ritual. This relationship is a ray. When you consider another card from the viewpoint of your significator, energy is transmitted from you, via your significator card, to the person, place, or thing that the other card represents. The ray will form itself automatically, but how potent it becomes and how effectively its force is used depends on several factors.

The potency of a ray hinges in large measure on how well you can enter your significator. The more completely you feel and believe yourself inside the significator court card, the more forcefully your awareness will extend from it. Also important is the strength of will that you use to project the ray. There is a great difference between simply reaching out to touch another card with your mind, and thrusting your will outward to that card, and indeed through it, like a psychic lance. Your power of concentration will determine how strongly you are able to hurl forth this lance of will.

The forcefulness of the ray can be increased by desire. Rituals involve inflaming the magical desire, and then releasing it toward its object so that at the moment of release, the magician becomes completely empty and passive, without desire of any kind. The desire is sent along the ray to its object, where it works its effect. After it is released, it ceases to be a part of the magician, just as an arrow fired from a bow ceases at once to be in contact with the archer, but becomes a part of its target.

When the purpose of a ritual is important to you personally, desire for its fulfillment will often be strong in a natural way, and will not require building up by artificial means. This natural desire can be used effectively provided that you do not brood over it and exhaust its energies in your imagination prior to the ritual. If you allow a natural desire to sustain itself as an unconsidered, raw force, feeling it seethe within you but making no attempt to define or limit it, that natural desire can be released along a ray with great success.

Dwelling on your desire in your mind by imagining its fulfillment is like repeatedly short-circuiting a battery. Eventually the sparks cease as the battery loses all of its power. You are left with the empty shell of desire. It has the same shape as your original desire, but there is no passion, only lifeless patterns of thought. Desire can be kept strong by holding it in the back of the mind without ever analyzing it. Be aware of it but do not think about it, or visualize its fulfillment, until the time for its ritual release.

Effective use of the ray is one of the most important skills in magic, but it is seldom mastered or even understood. Every ray has a beginning and an end point. In Tarot magic these points are represented by individual cards. The beginning point will usually be the significator of the magician. The end point may in theory be any other card, but in practice when deliberately projecting a ray it will most likely be either another court card or a number card.

A common ray carries force in one direction only. It is expressed in symbolic form by the Tarot emblem of the Sword, which is pointed on only one end, indicating the direction of force. A common ray is made by sending out a lance of will, and immediately turning the mind away from the purpose for which it is projected. In this way, nothing can rebound from the end point of the ray back upon the magician. This is why the ritual desire must be inflamed, projected, and in the act of projection, purged from the mind. A state of emptiness prevents a reflux along the ray. If the cards that form the start and end of the ray in a Tarot ritual are lifted from their places shortly after the ray is sent, a rebounding of force becomes impossible.

At times it is desirable to create a sustained communication along a ray from magician to the object of desire. This is called a reciprocating ray, and it is symbolized in the Tarot by the emblem of the Wand—a staff having in its most idealized form two equal and similar ends. A reciprocating ray is created by projecting the will along the ray, but leaving the mind aware of the purpose of the projection. That interest in the mind of the magician allows the reciprocal pulse that flows back along the projected ray to enter the mind and cause reaction. What returns along the ray is not the same as what is sent forth. It is colored and transformed by the nature of its object. However, it is equally powerful. The energy rebounds back and forth along a reciprocating ray, gradually transforming itself through interaction with the sender and the receiver.

Reciprocating rays can be used to establish relationships between two individuals, or between the magician and a topic or matter of interest, a place, a building, or indeed anything that the mind of the magician may wish to focus upon in a sustained manner, for the purpose of understanding it, appreciating it, enjoying it, transforming it, or even for acquiring a portion of its power.

The method of physically projecting a ray in Tarot magic is quite simple. Everything is done with the index finger of the right hand. By touching any card in a deliberate way with the tip of the right index finger, a point of focus is established. That card becomes resident within the mind of the magician. By touching a second card with the same fingertip, a ray is formed between the things represented by the two cards, and occult force flows outward from the thing the first card represents to the thing the second card represents. Casual touching of the cards does not project a ray of any efficacy, but only a deliberate touch with the intention of projecting the will.

For example, to send a ray of will outward from yourself to another individual, you would first touch your own significator with your right index finger, and then touch the significator of the other person. If the other's significator were directly below yours on the altar, a second touch would be given to your significator because two cards overlaid are symbolically already united. To create a reciprocating ray between yourself and a person or thing represented by a second card, you project a ray in the usual manner by touching your index finger to your significator, then touching the same finger to the other card, and again touching your own significator to indicate the returning pulse. The reciprocating ray is sustained by holding the relationship between the two cards in the mind, rather than simply ending the ritual.

EXERCISE OF THE RAY

Lay your significator upright on the table in front of you, and place a significator that represents another person you know well beside it, so that a card length separates the two cards. If the figure on your significator happens to face to one side or the other, place the second court card on whichever side causes your significator to look toward it. Project your awareness into your significator by imagining that you stand upon it as on a rug in the astral place of working. From this perspective upon the card, gaze across at the other card, which also lies on the floor like a rug, and visualize your friend standing on that card, looking back at you.

Touch the tip of your right index finger to your significator, and at the same time gather the force of your will. In the astral place of working, touch your right hand to the center of your chest. Touch with your right index finger the significator of the other person, and as you do so, project your will into the second card as though reaching out to touch the other person with your mind. Simultaneously on the astral level, use your right hand to grasp the light of your will in your heart center and cast it across at the person who stands upon the second card, as though you were throwing a bolt of lightning. A pulse of light extends from the middle of your chest and enters the chest of the other person in the astral space.

To indicate the initial returning pulse along the ray, touch your index finger to your significator card again, and visualize on the astral level that you touch the center of your chest with your right hand. Feel energy flow back along the ray into your heart center, then rebound to cycle back and forth with ever increasing rapidity from card to card, until the pulses blend together into a sustained ray. The beam of golden light extends from the heart center of your astral form to the heart center of the astral form of the other person as you both stand upon the enlarged cards.

Sustain this beam for several minutes on the astral level while gazing down at the significator of the other person on the table with your physical eyes. Open your mind to an awareness of your friend. If you wish, you can project your thoughts into that person's mind by mentally speaking to the person. When the effort to sustain the link with your friend begins to tire your mind, put away the cards to end the exercise. It is best not to tell your friend in advance that you are planning to work this exercise. Do not be surprised if the person informs you that he or she was thinking about you at the time of the exercise.

How much success you have in contacting your subject depends on many factors. Those who are psychically receptive will become aware of you and will think of you at the same time you do this exercise. Close friends, family members, or a lover are more likely to become aware of your contact than casual friends. Some times of day are more conducive to success than others. The best time is at night when the air is still, and when the cares of the day have been pressed to the background of the mind. If you do this exercise when your subject is asleep, that person may dream about you.

Too much straining of the mind on your part will not make the contact stronger, but will weaken it by inhibiting the free flow of the reciprocating pulse along the ray. The harder you try, the less you will achieve. This paradox of magic means that you are more likely to achieve success in early exercises, when you do not quite understand what you are doing. When you begin to think you have learned how to push out with your will with great force, you will find that success becomes more elusive, as you unconsciously block your own efforts.

Success will return once you learn to relax your mind and not strain with so much effort. The will must be projected firmly, but it cannot be forced. It must be allowed to flow with its own desire. You will know without a doubt that your exercise has been successful when your friend tells you later that he or she was thinking about you at the time of the exercise. Or that person may phone you at the time of the exercise or immediately after it. This happens with regularity when a true link has been made along the reciprocating ray. Indeed, you will become used to it and will eventually look upon it as an everyday occurrence.

There is no danger involved in this exercise. After all, you are only thinking about a person you know, which you do every day many times. However, when you do it in a ritual way using the symbolic tool of the reciprocating ray, and significator cards to focus and fix your own identity and the identity of your subject, the process is more likely to be perceived by the other person. In rare instances you will pick up the thoughts of your subject in words. This usually takes the form of a phrase or at most a few sentences. You may become aware of something they are considering in their mind, some subject that preoccupies their thoughts, in the form of images or even emotions. If you talk to the person soon after the exercise, be alert for anything the person may say that confirms that a connection was established.

It is an easy matter to end the exercise and break the ray between the two significators. Merely take them up from the table, return them to the Tarot deck, and shuffle the deck. Shuffling the deck erases the ritual structure and returns all of the cards to a chaotic state, destroying any associations they acquired during the ritual. It is equivalent to ceremonially cleansing a ritual object. The cards in a shuffled deck have no associations. They acquire them only when they are laid out during ritual, and will hold those associations for as long as the arrangement of the cards established during the ritual is sustained and preserved.

14

THE CIRCLE

The circle is the most powerful of all symbolic forms in ceremonial magic. Its use is virtually universal. You would be hard-pressed to find a system of magic in the world that does not use the circle, and always its basic meaning is the same—a barrier that defines a sacred space, and divides it from the rest of the world. Its shape is perfect, having no irregularity. In a geometric sense its perfection is expressed by its efficiency. The circle is the figure that encloses the largest possible area with the shortest possible circumference. The perfection of the circle, and its three-dimensional expression, the sphere, caused both to be regarded as divine by the ancient Greeks.

The number that expresses a circular shape in the history of Western culture is the number twelve. We can perceive this to be so by considering two structures that are related, the zodiac and the clock. The band surrounding the heavens was divided thousands of years ago by the Babylonians and Egyptians into twelve parts known as the zodiac. Since that time all astrological horoscopes have been similarly divided into twelve sections. This division found its reflection in the clock face, which in its early form of the sundial was divided into twelve parts to express the twelve hours of the day. The circle of the year is similarly divided into twelve months.

The circle of twelve parts is a celestial form. Whereas the surface of the Earth is divided into four, expressed by the four quarters and the four winds, the sky is divided into twelve, expressed by the zodiac signs. The cards forming the ritual circle are most naturally drawn from the trumps, because the trumps relate to heavenly matters and the circle is a heavenly form. It is not difficult to locate which trumps to use when it is remembered that the Greater Arcana has a group of twelve trumps linked to the twelve Single letters of the Hebrew alphabet, and that in the system of the Golden Dawn these trumps are assigned to the signs of the zodiac. Indeed, it is impossible to imagine another set of cards that embodies the ritual circle so perfectly.

Lay out the twelve trumps of the Greater Arcana that are linked with the twelve astrological signs in a ring face up so that the tops of all the cards point outward, and the bottoms point inward to the center. The bottom corners of the cards should touch but not overlap. This makes it easy to form them into a regular circular shape, and precisely defines the size of the circle. Having the cards touch is also a symbolic way to express the continuity of the magic circle.

It is best not to use a Tarot deck with very long and narrow cards when doing Tarot magic, because the odd proportions of the cards create a cramped circle with which to surround the altar. Any regular Tarot deck with cards of the usual proportions will result in a circle of a nearly perfect dimension for the use of that deck. Smaller card decks are to be preferred for ritual work since they take up less space on the table. They allow the ritual structure to be laid out in a very limited area. However, if you have a spacious working surface and do not mind stretching your arm, a deck of large cards works just as well.

Emperor (Aries)

Hierophant (Taurus)

Lovers (Gemini)

Chariot (Cancer)

Strength (Leo)

Hermit (Virgo)

Justice (Libra)

Death (Scorpio)

Temperance (Sagittarius)

Devil (Capricorn)

Star (Aquarius)

Moon (Pisces)

This list shows the Golden Dawn correspondences between the signs of the zodiac and the twelve trumps that are linked to the Single Hebrew letters. It is widely accepted, and is a good arrangement to use if you are just becoming acquainted with ritual magic. I do not wish to complicate this book with variations on this sequence, so I will use the Golden Dawn arrangement throughout. In my personal system of magic, I have made several changes to the sequence and correspondences of the trumps. Those who may be interested in my changes to the Golden Dawn correspondences will find them explained in the appendix.

For general purposes, the natural order of the signs works well enough in the circle, although there are other possible ways to sequence the cards. Begin at Aries in the east and lay out the cards clockwise in the traditional series of the signs: Aries, Taurus, Gemini, and so on, ending with Pisces. The trumps are laid out in a direction that is opposite the usual direction. The result is a mirror reflection of the circle of the zodiac. Symbolically, the zodiac has been drawn down from the sky and laid upon the earth, which causes its reversal, and has been rotated to place Aries in the east.

You should lay out the circle and study it, making yourself familiar with the arrangement of the zodiacal trumps, and with the sign that is linked to each card. In some Tarot decks that follow the system of the Golden Dawn, such as the Thoth deck of Aleister Crowley, the signs of the zodiac are printed on the faces of these twelve trumps. However, with traditional decks it is necessary to memorize the relationship so that you can lay the cards out quickly and with confidence.

NORTH

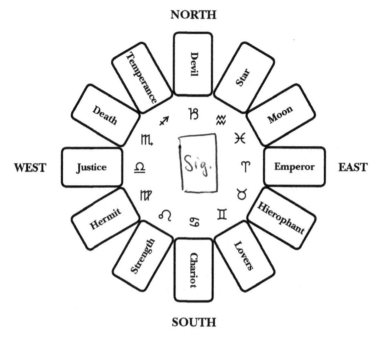

WEST — **EAST**

SOUTH

Circle of Zodiacal Trumps

EXERCISE OF THE CIRCLE

The laying out of the circle serves as an excellent preliminary ritual exercise when learning to work Tarot magic. It demonstrates the general way of projecting the circle that will be used in more complex rituals, and is a good way to memorize the signs that are linked to the zodiacal trumps.

Before you set down any other cards, the court significator you have chosen to represent yourself should be placed face up on the surface of the table, and upright from your perspective. When working more formal rituals it is placed upon the altar, but for the purpose of this exercise it is sufficient to place it alone upon the table. Lay the circle around it clockwise, beginning in the east with Aries and ending with Pisces. The circle in the illustration is shown from the perspective of the south, which is the usual way maps are presented, but it does not matter which side of the circle you sit on, only that the trump of the Emperor, linked to Aries, is placed in the east. There is really no best quarter to sit when practicing Tarot magic, but you may find visualization easier if you habitually sit in the west, facing the east with the circle in front of you on the table.

After all the trumps of the circle have been laid out, visualize yourself standing at the center of the circle upon the significator card you have chosen for yourself, facing east. As much as possible, you must transfer your point of view into the astral space occupied by the significator. Imagine that the significator is a rug about six feet long with the picture of the court card woven in great detail into its surface, and that you stand on that rug. Do not think of yourself as shrinking to stand upon the significator card on the tabletop, but rather imagine that the cards occupy another dimension of reality, the astral working space with the black floor, and that when you enter the circle you go to that place in your astral body where the cards are as large as you.

Visualize each trump of the zodiac as a brightly colored rug that lies flat upon the surface of the ritual space. See floating in the air above them twelve upright, glowing rectangles of golden light that are around the size of doorways. The lower edge of each rectangle floats a foot above the center of the card it represents. With your right index finger, touch your significator card. Imagine that you stand on the rug of the card in the astral place of working, and that you touch your own chest over your heart with your right hand. Speak the words:

"The All in One."

Touch with your right index finger each of the cards of the circle briefly in turn, beginning with Aries and proceeding clockwise around the circle to Pisces. As you touch each zodiacal trump, speak its name:

**"The Emperor, the Hierophant, the Lovers,
the Chariot, Strength, the Hermit, Justice, Death,
Temperance, the Devil, the Star, the Moon."**

As you utter the name of each trump, pause for a short time and imagine that you stand on your significator at the center of the circle, and point with your right hand at the rectangle of light above that trump in the circle. Mentally project from your index finger into the middle of the rectangle the sign of the zodiac that is linked with that card. The zodiac signs are shown in the center of the illustration. Visualize the symbol of the sign appearing in golden light to float upon the air above the card within its rectangle. The color resembles sunlight, and stands forth strongly against the darkness of the astral space.

A second time, touch the Emperor with your right index finger, and speak the words:

"The circle is complete."

Again, touch the significator at the center. As you do so, imagine that you touch your chest over your heart with your right hand while standing upon the card in the astral place of ritual. Say the words:

"The One in All."

Visualize a continuous ring of golden light expand itself from the point of your heart center outward all around you through the air to the rectangles at the level of their zodiac signs, so that the twelve signs float upon this ring of radiance. Contemplate the joined zodiacal circle that surrounds you.

To end this exercise, simply return your awareness to your physical body and gather up the cards on the table in the reverse order to which they were laid out. It is best to take up the cards one at a time. When you have them together in your hands, shuffle them into the rest of the pack. This removes any ritual associations they may have picked up during the exercise.

If the layout of your circle is slightly irregular, or if some of the bottom corners of the trumps do not touch the other cards, or are moved slightly away from the other cards during the exercise, do not be concerned. What is important is that in your imagination you see the ring of card rugs on the floor of the ritual place surrounding you in a perfect circle, and that all the corners of the cards in this imaginary circle touch and remain in contact for the entire duration of the ritual. The material world is imperfect, the ideal world is perfect. You can never create perfection with the physical cards, and do not need to try, but you can conceive perfection in your mind.

15

THE TRIANGLE

The triangle, and its three-dimensional counterpart the pyramid, have a long history in Western occultism as symbolic tools for actualizing what exists only in a potential form. The triangle does this by virtue of its shape—two sides diverge and expand from a single point down to a base. What exists only in potential is drawn through the gateway of the expanded point at the apex, represented graphically by the expanding sides of the triangle. When it reaches the solid and stable base, it becomes real. The same mechanism works in the opposite way just as effectively. What exists within the triangle can be made to diminish upward toward the apex and vanish through the gateway of the point from the manifest world to the unmanifest world.

The best example of the way the triangle was used in ancient times to banish is the ancient abracadabra charm. The word "abracadabra" is a real magic word, although it has been treated as a joke often in films, on television, and in books. It is a charm against fever and is always used in conjunction with a triangle, which may or may not surround the word, but which is always formed by the letters of the word itself. It was used by Serenus Sammonicus, physician to the Roman Emperor Caracalla (ruled 211–217), who was said to have invented the charm, but it has its origin much earlier in ancient Mesopotamia, and may derive from the Chaldean phrase *abbada ke dabra*, which translates to "perish like the word" (Budge, *Amulets and Talismans*, 220).

```
ABRACADABRA
ABRACADABR
ABRACADAB
ABRACADA
ABRACAD
ABRACA
ABRAC
ABRA
ABR
AB
A
```

The letters of the word are written in a row, then centered below it the same letters are written minus the last, then below the second row the same letters minus the last two, and so on until only a single letter remains. This creates the shape of an inverted triangle, and symbolically passes the word, which is identified magically with the fever itself, from the base through the point doorway at the apex of the inverted triangle and out of the manifest world of real existence. The charm is activated by chanting the diminishing word. As the word is expelled, so is the fever. Other charms were used in the same way, to banish what was unwanted. The abracadabra charm is merely the best known.

The triangle can also be used to bring forth into actual being that which exists only in a potential or ideal form. When used in this way, it is formed upright from the perspective of the user. This was the practice of medieval magicians, who summoned demons into the ritual triangle outside the boundary of their magic circle, which protected them from the malice of the spirits. A triangle was always inscribed on the floor or ground of the working space when lower spirits were evoked to visible appearance. The triangle of evocation is as much a part of traditional European magic as the circle itself, and most true grimoires include it.

In Tarot magic, a triangle is used to actualize the ritual purpose. It is formed beside the circle and points away from the circle, as in traditional spirit evocation. The mechanism of actualization has two parts. It involves sending the ritual purpose, as symbolically expressed by the cards that rest upon the triangle, through the apex as a pulse of will to the unmanifest or ideal level, where that purpose is immediately reflected back down into the manifest world in the form of realization. This reflection of the purpose happens automatically.

This mechanism is identical to that used by the abracadabra charm, although its full structure may not have been understood by those who employed the charm. The energy of the charm, symbolically represented by the word, is sent out through the apex of the triangle by the diminishing of the word to a single letter, and that magical purpose is immediately reflected back into the greater world as the realization of the purpose of the charm, which is the ending of the fever. What was enacted within the triangle in symbolic form becomes realized in the greater world in actual form. The trigger of the actualization is passage of the energy through the point gateway of the triangle, and its reflected pulse.

The ritual triangle is really a fixed and static representation of the vortex, a turning three-dimensional spiral. When an intention that is represented in symbolic form within the ritual space is projected using the power of the will, it is invariably projected through a vortex, even though those who project it are not always aware of this process. It is the vortex created by the projected force of the will that lifts the purpose expressed by the ritual out of the everyday material world, where it would remain powerless, and sends it into the potential or ideal world, where it is immediately reflected back into the material world as the purpose realized.

It is not necessary to understand the theory behind the use of the vortex in ritual in order to successfully work Tarot magic. All you need to know is that the purpose of a ritual is represented by the cards you place on top of the triangle, and that during the ritual you focus your intention through the triangle with that purpose strongly held in your mind. Your projected willpower itself opens a vortex to the unmanifest world automatically, but the gateway is facilitated by the shape of the physical triangle of trumps. What is sent into the higher world always returns, immediately reflected to the lower world and realized, though the realization is not always at once apparent, and it does not always take the expected form. Time may pass before the realization is able to express itself on the material level.

Among the trumps that provide the structure for rituals of Tarot magic, there is a group that is naturally best suited to create the triangle: the three elemental trumps of the Mother letters of the Hebrew alphabet. In the cosmological model upon which the Tarot correspondences of the Golden Dawn are based, the higher elements, Fire, Air, and Water, lie in bands between the sphere of the fixed Earth and the higher-moving spheres of the heavens. They partake of both earthly and heavenly qualities. They are above the surface of the earthly sphere, yet they have lower, earthly counterparts that function within the sphere of Earth. Hence they are ideally suited to create a bridge between the potential and the actual, and for forming the symbolic tool that causes the ideal to be made real.

To form the triangle of realization, first set down the Fool at one of the four cardinal points approximately a card-length away from the circle, so that the base of the Fool points toward the center of the circle. Next, set the Hanged Man so that its base touches and halfway overlaps the left side of the base of the Fool, at an angle of 120° to the Fool. Finally, set Judgement so that its base is beneath the base of the Fool, but on top of the base of the Hanged Man, angled 120° away from the other two trumps.

This arrangement is more complicated to describe in words than it is to lay out. The bases of all three cards touch and interweave in such a way that there is almost no space at their center, and so that the tops of the cards define the points of a triangle. This figure is called a *triskelion,* which simply means "three-legged." The cards will be slightly tipped and elevated above the surface of the table by their interaction if you use a smaller deck. They form a kind of propeller shape that, if set into clockwise rotation would cause the triangle to rise, but if rotated counterclockwise would cause the triangle to descend. The tiny space at the center of the triangle is itself triangular, but it points in a direction opposite the triangle

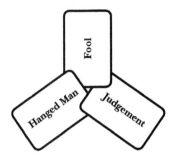

Triangle of Realization

that is defined by the tops of the three trumps. The accompanying diagram will be easier to understand than the description.

The Fool, with its designation of zero, serves as the portal in Tarot magic. It is through the Fool that ritual desire is projected and psychic links established. Air is the element of the mind, and the Fool represents the higher zone of spiritual Air that encircles the world and mediates between the bands of spiritual Fire (Judgement) above it, and spiritual Water (Hanged Man) below it. The Hebrew letter linked with the Fool, Aleph, and its corresponding element Air, are said in *Sepher Yetzirah* to be "as the tongue of a balance standing between these contraries [Fire and Water] which are in equilibrium, reconciling and mediating between them" (Westcott, 18).

The triskelion may be thought of as a balance that can tip in either direction to create opposite vortices that turn either clockwise or counterclockwise. The two sides are never separated, being part of the same structure. Projection of a ritual purpose through the triangle creates a clockwise-inward spiral; the reflected pulse that actualizes the purpose takes the form of a counterclockwise-outward spiral. It is not necessary to actually form spirals during rituals of Tarot magic—thanks to the use of the triangle of trumps, they form themselves automatically.

Which cardinal direction the triangle points toward will depend on the purpose of the ritual. It should be placed in the east, south, west, or north, to correspond with the element that best accords with the ritual objective. When only a single realizer card is placed on the triangle, the triangle should point in the direction that corresponds with the suit of that card.

Works of dominance, initiative, command, boldness, the exercise of authority, or great haste would be in harmony with a southern triangle, since the south is the quarter of elemental Fire.

Works of love, friendship, the affections, social activities, romance, the family, or deep feelings would require a western placement of the triangle since the west is the quarter of elemental Water.

Works of aggression, malice, competition, conflict, argument, debate, analysis, dissection, investigation, or punishment invite an eastern triangle since the east is the quarter of elemental Air in the Golden Dawn system.

Works of labor, growth, accumulation, strengthening, healing, nourishment, cultivation, a place of employment, or the home invite a northern triangle since the north is the quarter of elemental Earth.

EXERCISE OF THE TRIANGLE

As a useful exercise in the construction of the triangle of realization, choose a number card other than an Ace that expresses some realization you wish to achieve in your life. Set your significator court card face up on the table in front of you so that it is upright from your point of view. It serves as the center from which you orient the triangle. Build the triangle on the table about a card-length away from the significator above, below, on the left, or on the right of it, so that the Fool points toward the quarter matching the suit of the chosen card—east for Swords, south for Wands, west for Cups, and north for Pentacles.

Lay the realizer card you have selected on top of the triangle in the middle so that it points in the same direction as the Fool. Do not worry if it is sideways or upside down from your perspective—it must be aligned with the Fool, which has its base pointing toward your significator. The number card is centered over the middle of the triangle, and covers around half of the Fool. Concentrate on the purpose you wish to achieve, imagining it in your mind as a thing in the process of becoming real. See its achievement clearly in your thoughts as though it were being acted out on stage or in a film.

At the same time, imagine you are standing in your astral body in the ritual place on top of the rug of your significator, looking at the three overlapping rugs that compose the triangle several paces away. They rest on a low dais that elevates them nine inches above the floor. It has the shape of a triangle with its points cut off.

In your physical body, touch in turn counterclockwise the three trumps of the triangle with your right index finger, saying as you do so:

"The Fool, the Hanged Man, Judgement."

Once again touch the Fool, closing the triangle, and say:

"The triangle is complete."

Visualize an upright triangle of white light form itself in the air above the triangular dais in the astral place of working. It floats a foot or so above the three rugs on the dais, and is six feet in height.

Gather your purpose in your mind and intensify it for a minute or so using the power of your will. With your right index finger, touch the middle of your significator card. At the same time, in your astral form as you stand before the triangle, lay your right hand over your chest. Speak the words:

"The purpose is willed."

Touch the center of the card on the triangle of trumps that you have chosen to express the realization of your will with your fingertip, and in your astral form cast your entire right hand at the center of the glowing triangle of light as though throwing a bolt of force from your chest into the triangle, saying:

"The purpose is fulfilled."

Cast your desire like a shining lance out of your chest with your right hand and through the middle of the glowing triangle that floats on the air, so that the triangle fills with its expanded blinding radiance. Your right hand should direct its course as it darts out of the center of your chest. Contemplate the brightness that fills the triangle for several seconds, then allow the intense glow to fade as you release all desire and doubt from your mind, and turn your thoughts away from your intention. Relax completely. Pretend to yourself that whatever you wished to accomplish is a thing already done that does not require any further attention. Mentally, you must turn your back upon it.

Gather up the cards one by one in the reverse order to which they were laid out and shuffle them into the deck. Taking up the cards closes the portal of the triangle. Shuffling them removes any specific associations they have acquired during the ritual.

16

THE CROSS

In religion as in magic, the altar was traditionally considered to be essential in bridging the gulf between the world of spirit and the world of matter. It was the instrument of interaction with the gods. Sacrifices made on the altars of the ancient peoples were dedicated to the ruling spiritual beings, who in return sent their power down into the altars, and through the altars, for the benefit of the worshippers. The offering of sacrifice created a vortex of desire above the altar top, and this was answered by an opposite vortex of realization.

In general form, altars are usually cubic or oblong, having a flat top and four sides. An altar is the center of the sacred space that contains it, whether that is a church, a hilltop, or a magic circle. This is true even if the altar is not located in the center of the circle. The altar is naturally the focus of the circle. Its square shape suggests its immobility—the center is always fixed and unmoving because it is the reference point around which all other things move. Its shape also expresses the weight or tangibility of the altar. It represents the manifestation and realization of spiritual or sacred power in the physical world. It is not accidental that the seat of the throne of a king is often cubic or roughly cubic in shape. The throne is the symbol of the manifest power of the king. The shape of the throne mimics the shape of an altar, because the seat of the king is the seat of God. The king was viewed as God's representative on earth who ruled by divine right.

In ritual, the physical body of the magician may take the place of a separate altar, if the magician stands at the center of the empty magic circle. The ability to substitute the human body for an altar has been used in Tarot magic, where the significator of the magician, representing his astral body, is placed on top of the altar, which has the form and function of a raised stage. The altar is not completely displaced by the body of the magician, but the body of the magician becomes the focus for ritual energies upon the stage of the altar.

The elemental cross serves as the altar of Tarot magic. Because of the shape of the cards, it is easy and natural to build an altar of four cards as a cross, but awkward to build it in the form of a square. When laid as a square, the bases of the four interlaced cards cannot converge at the center, a necessary feature of the altar because it emphasizes the center point as the point of emanation. The cross creates an altar of perfect size to fit within the circle of the zodiacal trumps, but an altar based on the square is smaller and less esthetically pleasing when set in the circle.

The square and the cross are intimately connected, so that the existence of one naturally implies the existence of the other. The points of an equal-armed cross when joined by lines define a square, and lines drawn through the corners of a square across the center define a cross. The practice of setting the four elemental instruments upon the surface of the altar in Golden Dawn rituals draws a cross on the altar through its center, defining in this way the center point of the altar, and of the circle in which the altar is set. The use of the cross as the altar in Tarot magic accomplishes the same purpose. It locates the center point of the circle.

During rituals the magician will usually stand in the middle of the altar on the astral level, the central position represented physically by the central placement of the significator. However, the cross shape of the altar in Tarot magic has the advantage of allowing the magician to occupy one of its arms on the astral level in order to work magic that uses the power of only a single element—the evocation of an elemental spirit, for example. This deliberately created imbalance is represented physically by shifting the significator toward the arm of the cross that corresponds with the elemental magic being worked.

In full rituals, the elemental altar has the distinction of being erected in the working space first, before any other cards are laid. Symbolically, it is the zone of the four lower elements and must be created as a firm foundation upon which to build the rest of the ritual structures. It is also the elevated platform upon which the significator representing the magician resides during ritual, and so must be brought into existence before the significator can be placed.

The four Aces of the suits compose the cross. They are arranged with their bottom edges touching and overlapping, so that their top edges point outward to the four directions of the compass. The relationship of the Aces to the four directions is that used in the Golden Dawn system of magic for the four elemental instruments—Swords and elemental Air in the east, Wands and elemental Fire in the south, Cups and elemental Water in the west, Pentacles and elemental Earth in the north. Other arrangements are possible (refer to the appendix), but for the sake of simplicity the Golden Dawn system is used throughout the text.

It may seem strange that the Aces represent the four manifest elements since the Aces reside on the Tree of Life in Kether, the highest of the ten Sephiroth. At first consideration, the four Tens might appear to be a better choice. However, the Tens have specific and limited meanings, whereas the Aces are the roots and upwelling sources for the elemental energies of the suits, embodying within themselves in potential all the meanings of the number cards of their suits. In the Kabbalah, Kether and Malkuth are esoterically connected, since the Malkuth of a higher world is the Kether of a lower world. The Aces (01) and Tens (10) are also intimately connected, as the mirror reflection of their numbers suggests.

Lay first the Ace of Swords so that its upper edge points toward the east. Second, lay upon it the Ace of Wands pointing toward the south so that half the base of the card touches and overlaps

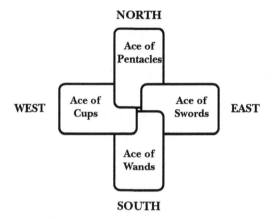

The Cross of the Altar

half the base of the Ace of Swords. The two cards will be at a right angle to each other. Thirdly, lay the Ace of Cups pointing toward the west in such a way that half the base of the card touches and overlaps half the base of the Ace of Wands. It will be at a right angle to the Ace of Wands. Finally, lay the Ace of Pentacles pointing toward the north so that half its base touches and overlaps half the base of the Ace of Cups. The other half of the base of the Ace of Pentacles is slid under half the base of the Ace of Swords.

The diagram will make this arrangement of the four Aces plain at a glance. Each Ace points toward the compass direction associated with its element in the Golden Dawn. The interweaving of the bases causes all four cards to stand up from the table slightly. This tilting of the cards is scarcely noticeable with larger decks but still exists in the overlap of the bases. It is this elevation that provides the altar for the significator, and at least in a symbolic way raises the significator above the other cards of the ritual. If you use a smaller deck of cards, you will notice that the effect is more pronounced than the similar elevation produced by interweaving the bases of the cards of the triangle. At the center where they join is a small square hole, the point center of the altar and of the ritual circle.

It will be found that with Tarot cards of the usual proportions—for example, the standard Rider-Waite deck—the circle of the zodiac trumps is almost exactly the correct size to enclose the four Aces of the altar. The elegance of this relationship is at once apparent when the circle is laid out around the cross. No space is wasted within the circle, and the ritual layout of the cards is rendered as compact as it could possibly be made, so that it takes up the least area on the working surface for a given deck of Tarot cards. A deck of large cards will require a bigger working space than a deck of small cards, but the efficiency of the layout is preserved in either case.

EXERCISE OF THE CROSS

The altar may be used in conjunction with the significator to perform a simple centering exercise. The circle and triangle are not required. Build the cross of the altar in the manner described and lay your significator on top of it so that the significator is centered on the cross, and upright from your perspective. It does not matter which of the four directions the significator points toward as long as it is upright to you.

Imagine that the four cards of the altar are rugs each six feet long, bearing beautifully detailed images of the Aces. These rugs rest upon an elevated dais in the shape of a cross with equal arms that is twelve inches above the level of the floor. The astral dais of the triangle, which is not used in this exercise, is elevated nine inches above the floor, but the astral dais of the altar, twelve inches. Visualize yourself standing upon the significator rug in the center of the dais, facing east with your arms spread wide so that your body forms a great cross. It may help you to visualize this if you sit in the west, so that you are physically facing east during the exercise.

With your right index finger, touch the significator and say the words:

"The heart of the four."

Touch in turn the Ace of Swords, the Ace of Cups, the Ace of Pentacles, and the Ace of Wands, so that the movement of your finger describes a cross. As you touch the four cards, say the words:

"The Sword before me, the Cup behind me, the Pentacle on my left hand, the Wand on my right hand."

Pause a moment when you touch each card. As you name the emblem of the Sword, visualize in the astral place of working a glowing sword in front of you, floating point upwards on the air above the top edge of the Ace of Swords in the east. As you name the Cup, picture a glowing cup floating behind you above the top edge of the Ace of Cups to the west. As you name the Pentacle, imagine a glowing pentacle above the top edge of the Ace of Pentacles in the north. As you name the Wand, imagine a glowing wand above the top edge of the Ace of Wands in the south. These symbolic forms float at the heart level of your astral body, above the outer ends of the four arms of the cross that is the altar, at the edges of the raised dais.

Touch your significator with your fingertip, and say the words:

"The center of the universe."

See in your mind four rays of light extending outward from your heart center to pierce the four elemental symbols of the suits, so that you stand with arms spread wide in the center of a cross of golden light. Feel yourself centered in the universe, and extend the beams of the cross endlessly away in the four directions of space. Allow them to fade slowly. Gather up the cards in the reverse order to the way they were laid out, and shuffle them back into the deck to remove any ritual associations from them.

17

GENERAL METHOD
OF TAROT RITUAL

Every full ritual starts with a blank working surface large enough to hold the complete ritual layout. This will usually be a table, but any flat surface will serve the same purpose. It is one of the great virtues of Tarot magic that the cards can be laid out anywhere, on anything. Whatever the physical surface, the corresponding astral place of working should be visualized in the imagination as a featureless black floor that extends in all directions into darkness, at least in the beginning stages of your practice. By eliminating extraneous distractions from the astral landscape, the attention is more easily concentrated on the various details of the ritual.

Later, when you have mastered the technique of creating an astral space, you can, if you wish, modify it to match your own inclinations. It is possible to make the astral workspace into anything you imagine—a mountain top, a field, a cathedral, a cavern, a pyramid, a special room, whatever best aids you in achieving success with your rituals.

It is important to grasp the underlying concept of a physical workspace that is overlaid by an astral workspace. The two coexist, and magic is done on both levels simultaneously. Indeed, there is an even more elevated working space of the spirit, but it is not necessary to hold this in the mind while doing rituals because it forms itself automatically to reflect the astral level.

In ordinary Western ceremonial magic, the astral space is usually of the same dimension as the physical place in which the ritual is worked, and often has roughly the same appearance. For example, a ritual might be worked in a room on which a magic circle has been drawn on the floorboards with chalk. The chalk line is only the material model for the magic circle, which does not really come into being until it is created in the astral space by the imagination. The astral circle is visualized in the astral equivalent to the physical room as a glowing band of light that floats upon the air at heart level above the physical circle of chalk. Both are held in the mind, which dances from one to the other and in this way sustains them. The magician is aware of the chalk circle, and also of the glowing astral circle above it.

All magic is worked on the astral plane, but the physical plane is needed to give solidity and persistence to astral forms. A magician who tries to work strictly in the astral environment is likely to have poorer results than one who bases his astral tools upon material tools that he can pick up and handle. That is the purpose of the cards in Tarot magic. They anchor the astral forms that are associated with them, giving the astral forms a power that only comes from matter. The physical world has many limitations, but it has one great virtue—its inertia. Physical matter persists on its own without effort. It does not need to be sustained or constantly reinforced. The physical Tarot cards act as a supporting foundation of matter for the astral forces and shapes that are manipulated on the astral level during ritual.

Tarot magic is somewhat different from most types of Western ceremonial magic in that its physical tools do not correspond as closely in size and shape with its astral tools. Whereas in Golden Dawn magic, for example, the astral cup is a close representation of the physical cup that is held in the hand, in Tarot magic the astral cup is represented on the physical level only by a much smaller image printed on a piece of cardboard. The physical circle is too small to stand within, but it can be entered on the astral level where its dimensions are easily expanded.

There is a lot of nonsense written about the astral realm, perhaps in part because the name itself is so misleading. It is also variously referred to as the astral plane, the astral level, the astral world, the astral dimension, or simply as the astral. The word *astral* means of or like the stars. However, the stars have little to do with the astral realm, which is simply a world or environment that holds form but no substance. In the Kabbalah, it corresponds with the ninth emanation, Yesod, which is linked with the Moon. We enter the astral realm in dreams, and less perfectly during daydreams or when we imagine. It is the place where human beings and spiritual beings can most easily meet and interact. Magicians deliberately enter and manipulate the astral realm. The ability to do so is one of the most important skills of magic. It can only be learned through practice.

What follows is the general outline for the full ritual method of Tarot magic. Think of it as a template that gives the overall pattern for the average ritual. You should not feel that you must remain rigidly bound to it. The ritual structure is modular, and flexible, as the exercises you have already performed have demonstrated. The words spoken are provided as workable examples, but there is no magic power inherent in these particular words. Their purpose is to direct and focus the mind from step to step during the ritual, guiding the consciousness toward the fulfillment of its purpose.

THE RITUAL METHOD

First to be erected is the altar of the elements, which is the elevated stage for the significator. It must be built before the significator can occupy it. Think of the working surface as the endless sea of primordial chaos, and the altar as a firm ledge of rock that rises above the surface of those waters. It is the first tangible thing to be formed in the ritual process. It arises from the central point where the bases of the cards touch and overlap. All points are the same, being without dimension and undifferentiated, and in this sense all are connected. The point at the center of the altar of the

significator is connected with the point at the center of the interwoven cards of the triangle of realization that will be formed later.

After the altar has been prepared, the significator representing
the magician is placed upon it. During this placement, the point
of view of the magician should be transferred into the significator,
so that he or she seems to stand with arms spread wide and facing
the east upon an elevated dais in the shape of a cross. Each arm
of this dais should be imagined to have a rug laid on its surface,
each rug bearing the colorful and finely detailed image of an Ace.

Touch your significator with your right index finger, then touch
in turn the Ace of Swords, Ace of Cups, Ace of Pentacles, and
Ace of Wands, so that your finger describes a cross through the
significator. Visualize in the astral place the four symbols of the
suits glowing in the air at heart level above the upper edges of the
altar cards, at the edges of the dais. Touch the significator again,
and visualize a cross of light extending in four directions outward
from your heart center to pass through the four suit symbols.

The following words for this centering part of the general ritual should be spoken:

"The heart of the four." (touch significator)

**"The Sword before me, the Cup behind me, the Pentacle on my
left hand, the Wand on my right hand."** (touch each Ace in turn)

"The center of the universe." (touch significator)

Visualize yourself lowering your arms to your sides as you
stand upon the altar of the Aces, contemplating the light of the
cross as its brightness slowly fades.

Having energized the altar of the elements and established yourself at the center of the universe, the next task is to enclose the altar within a magic circle. Lay out the circle of the zodiac trumps
clockwise, beginning in the east with the Emperor (Aries). When
the circle has been completed, conceive doorways of light floating
in the air above each trump of the circle. With your right index
finger, touch the significator, then each of the zodiacal trumps in

turn beginning with the Emperor. Touch the Emperor again, and then touch the significator again. As you touch the cards, speak the following words:

"The One in All." (touch significator)

"The Emperor, the Hierophant, the Lovers, the Chariot, Strength, the Hermit, Justice, Death, Temperance, the Devil, the Star, the Moon." (touch each trump in turn)

"The circle is complete." (touch Emperor)

"The All in One." (touch significator)

When you tap your significator, touch your chest with your right hand on the astral level. As you speak the name of each trump, visualize yourself standing upon the altar, and point with your right hand at the rectangle of light above the trump. The utterance of the name of the trump causes the symbol of its zodiac sign to appear within the rectangle. When you physically touch the significator a second time with your index finger, again touch your chest with your right hand in the astral realm and imagine a circle of golden light expanding from the heart center of your astral form within the circle to link all twelve signs as it floats upon the air above the zodiacal trumps at heart level.

The ritual circle is further empowered and defined by the use of planetary modifiers. These are the seven trumps linked in the Golden Dawn system of correspondences with the seven traditional wandering bodies of astrology. Tarot magic can be worked without them, but their skillful use makes its rituals more effective. By placing one or more of the planetary trumps on top of the zodiacal trumps, the circle becomes energized by those ruling planets. A planetary modifier is laid directly over a trump of a sign so that it completely covers that card, with its base pointing toward the center of the circle.

There is no single instruction for the placement of planetary modifiers upon the zodiacal trumps. A modifier card should usually be located on top of the card of a sign its planet rules. This is the safest and most rational way to position them, but there is nothing to prevent any modifier from being placed on any sign. We will examine them in greater detail in later chapters. When a planetary trump is laid on the circle, the symbol of the planet is visualized within the rectangle of light that floats above the zodiacal card on which it is placed, and the name of the planetary trump spoken aloud. The rectangle of light will contain both the symbol of the zodiac sign and above it, the symbol of the planet.

Lay out the triangle of realization beside the circle with its trumps interwoven at their bases as already described. Build it in the quarter next to the Ace that has the greatest harmony with the purpose of the ritual. If only a single card is to be placed on the triangle, whether it is a court or number card, the triangle should usually be established in the quarter that matches the suit of that card. If there is both a court card and a number card, the triangle will be located in the quarter corresponding with the suit of the number card; but if two or more number cards of different suits occupies the triangle, the quarter where the triangle is located must be chosen according to its general harmony with the purpose of the ritual.

From the viewpoint of the significator upon the altar, visualize the three trumps of the triangle as rugs, each around six feet long, lying flat on a raised dais that is in the shape of a triangle with its points cut off. This dais is nine inches above the floor, not quite so high as the dais of the altar cross which is twelve inches above the floor.

The final card of the full ritual layout is the card of the Minor Arcana that acts as the focus for the ray of will from the altar. It is placed upon the center of the triangle so that it is aligned with the Fool. This last card best embodies the object of the ritual desire. If the ritual is directed toward another human being, it will usually be a second significator that represents the other person, drawn from the remaining court cards. If the ritual is done to bring about a material change in something other than another human being,

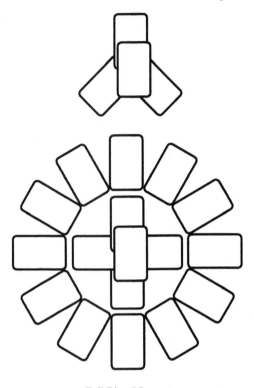

Full Ritual Layout

the card on the triangle will be a number card from Two to Ten of the suit that best expresses the purpose of the ritual.

The number cards other than the Aces are known as realizers because they realize or bring about the ritual fulfillment. As many as three realizer cards may be placed together in a stack on the triangle, although it is often best for the sake of clarity of purpose to use a single realizer. The cards on the triangle should never exceed three realizer cards plus an optional significator since the purpose of the ritual will become unfocused if more than three number cards are used.

To erect the triangle on the astral level, touch with your right index finger in turn the Fool, the Hanged Man, and Judgement, then once again the Fool to close and complete the triangle. These words are spoken as the cards are touched:

"The Fool, the Hanged Man, Judgement."
(three trumps of the triangle)

"The triangle is complete." (the Fool again)

Imagine an upright triangle of golden light form itself in the air above the reclining triangle of three rugs on the dais. The lines of the triangle draw themselves from the apex in a counterclockwise direction. Its base floats a foot above the dais, and it is six feet tall.

Fill your mind with awareness of your ritual purpose, and imagine that the circle on the astral level is charged to bursting with the energy of your desire. See it and feel it flickering around you as you stand upon the altar facing the triangle. Visualize this energy of desire begin to swirl in a clockwise vortex around the circle and form a funnel shape, like a miniature tornado of light, that has its focus upon your heart center.

Touch with your right index finger your significator in the center of the circle, and then the card upon the triangle. As you touch them, say the words:

"The purpose is willed." (significator)

"The purpose is fulfilled." (card of realization)

As you touch the significator, be fully aware of the energy of desire that fills your heart center, and imagine that you touch your chest with your right hand. As you touch the card of realization, on the astral level cast your right hand away from your chest toward the glowing triangle of light, releasing a bolt of blinding white radiance from your heart center and directing it with your hand through the center of the triangle. This lance composed of the force of your will pierces the upright triangle that floats in the air, so that the entire triangle fills and glows with brightness.

If this ritual involved the creation of a reciprocating ray, you would again touch with your index finger your own significator at the center of the circle, speaking the words:

"The way is open." (significator)

On the astral level, you would visualize a returning bolt of light that flies from the center of the triangle and passes into your chest, only to dart forth again into the triangle, then back into your heart center, moving more and more quickly until it is no longer a bolt of light but a beam that connects your astral body with the triangle.

More commonly, your ritual will be one designed to attain a goal rather than to sustain a link, and will involve an ordinary ray that is hurled forth with the strength of the aroused will, but not returned. When this is the case, the final line of the ritual is not spoken, but instead you at once empty your mind of desire and collect the cards in the reverse order to which they were laid out, shuffling them into the deck to cleanse them of ritual associations.

A reciprocating ray has a tendency to form itself automatically, without requiring the aid of additional visualization, when the start point and end point of the ray are sustained in the imagination. The energy you project along a ray of will during a ritual remains active for as long as the ritual layout rests undisturbed. There will be a reflux from the object of your desire through its realizer on the triangle to your own significator on the altar, and by association into your own mind. Unless you wish to commune or unite with the person or thing that is the focus of the ritual, it is best to shuffle the cards of the layout back into the deck immediately after finishing the ritual.

18

PLANETARY MODIFIERS

The circle of zodiacal trumps in the ritual layout is perfect, balanced, and unchanging. It is similar to the band of the heavenly zodiac when considered apart from the planets. All twelve zodiac signs exist in absolute harmony in the sphere of the fixed stars, so that no single sign expresses its individual nature at the expense of the others. In order for a sign to stand apart, it must be distinguished in some way. In astrology, this is accomplished by the planets moving against the backdrop of the stars. Planets interact with signs when they cross in front of them. Neither can be considered apart because a planet is always in one or another of the signs. A planet distinguishes the sign it occupies from the other signs, and the sign modifies the activity of the planet.

By placing a trump linked to a planet on top of the trump of a zodiac sign, the occult energies of the ritual circle may be deliberately unbalanced for specific purposes. The influence of that planet becomes emphasized, and it is easier to cause change in the areas of life affected by that planet and the sign it occupies. In a traditional astrological chart, all seven planets are always present, interacting with each other in an endless dance of the *aspects*—the angles the planets form with each other. All seven planetary trumps may be placed as modifiers on the zodiacal circle during a ritual, but it is usually best to limit their number, so that the clarity of their influence is maintained. The more modifiers used, the less important any one of them becomes.

Those just learning Tarot magic who have no knowledge of astrological symbolism are advised to work their first rituals without using planetary modifiers. Better that the action of the ritual be somewhat weaker than the wrong energies be applied due to ignorance of what the planets signify. Once you acquire a basic familiarity with the techniques of Tarot magic, you can add the planetary modifiers to the ritual mix by placing them on their ruling signs. Modifiers placed on their own signs will act with great purity and force. Almost any ritual purpose can be achieved by putting the trumps of the planets on the trumps of the signs they rule.

Only those with a confident understanding of astrology should locate the modifiers on signs they do not rule, because it is possible through error to frustrate the energies of the planets, or even to corrupt them, so that they bring about an undesirable effect. Modifiers are always placed directly over the trumps of the signs, so that the planetary trumps cover the zodiacal trumps beneath them. They are oriented with their bases pointing toward the center of the circle, as are the trumps of the signs.

All the traditional planets rule two signs each, except for the Sun and the Moon, which each rule only one sign. The planets added to modern astrology, Uranus, Neptune, and Pluto, have no place in the Golden Dawn correspondences for the trumps, which are based on traditional astrology.

Ruling Planet	Signs Ruled
Sun (Sun)	Strength (Leo)
High Priestess (Moon)	Chariot (Cancer)
Magician (Mercury)	Lovers (Gemini); Hermit (Virgo)
Empress (Venus)	Hierophant (Taurus); Justice (Libra)
Tower (Mars)	Emperor (Aries); Death (Scorpio)
Wheel (Jupiter)	Moon (Pisces); Temperance (Sagittarius)
World (Saturn)	Star (Aquarius); Devil (Capricorn)

The assignment of ruling planets to signs might appear haphazard at first glance, but it is based on a bilateral symmetry of the zodiac, which is divided into two halves called *sects*.

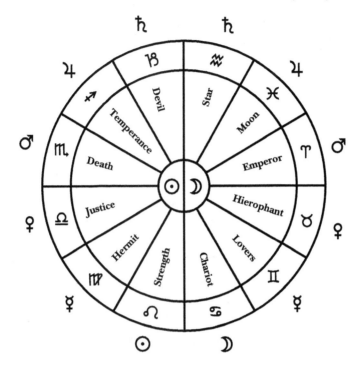

Solar and Lunar Sects of the Zodiac

The zodiac shown in the diagram has been reversed to accurately represent the zodiacal circle of trumps used in Tarot magic. In the usual diagram of the zodiac the order of signs (Aries, Taurus, Gemini, etc.) is counterclockwise, but here the order is clockwise.

Do not feel that because the Golden Dawn system of magic uses only seven planets rather than ten that it is somehow inferior, or incomplete. If you look at the diagram of the solar and lunar sects, you will observe that there are no gaps. Traditional astrology is a complete and perfect system. It was used with confidence from the times of the ancient Egyptians and Greeks down to the discovery of the planet Uranus by William Herschel in 1781. The finding of the first outer planet must have been an unsettling event in the world of astrology. With the subsequent discovery of Neptune in 1846 and Pluto in 1930, modern astrologers felt the increasing need to modify astrology to accommodate the outer planets. In my own view, this was a mistake. There is nothing lacking in the system of traditional astrology, which needed only seven planets for a span of thousands of years.

It is not necessary for the beginner in Tarot magic to know the meanings of the signs and houses. More advanced magicians who have a background in astrology will consider the meanings of the signs and houses when placing the planetary modifiers freely on all twelve signs, but beginners only need to know that the action of a planet is stronger in the sign it rules. When you wish to add the force of a planet to a ritual, put its trump on the trump of its own sign. If beginners follow this general rule, the modifiers will strengthen the working of the ritual.

The question becomes, "Which of the two sects should the five lesser planets occupy?" For example, should the planetary trump the Magician, representing the active power of Mercury, be placed on the Lovers in the lunar sect, or on the Hermit in the solar sect? We don't need to ask this question of the greater planets, the Sun and Moon, since they rule only one sign each.

The sect into which the trump of a lesser planet is placed depends on whether it is desirable that its overall influence be solar or lunar. In general, if you wish its action to be overt, direct, or expansive, place the modifier in the solar sect; if you want its action to be more subtle, reflective, or restrictive, use the lunar sect.

Lunar	Solar
feminine	masculine
cyclic	constant
changeable	steady
temporary	enduring
receptive	radiant
cool	hot
moist	dry
shadowed	bright
emotional	rational
fecund	seminal
intuitive	inspirational
formative	creative

The areas of life influenced by the seven traditional planets that are listed briefly below will provide a starting place for beginners in the correct use of the planetary modifiers in Tarot rituals. The more that is understood about the planets, signs, and houses of astrology, the more accurately the modifiers may be placed.

Sun: works of completion, integration, wholeness, spiritual matters, centering, self-improvement, creativity, the father

Moon: cyclic functions, assimilation, health (mental and physical), dreams, deception, fantasy, instability, change, secret growth, personal possessions, the mother

Mercury: communication, commerce, interpretation, transportation, travel, translation, information, knowledge, eloquence, persuasion, a child or sibling

Venus: affection, sympathy, unity, acquisition, attraction, fertility, pregnancy, nurture, harmony, nature, nourishment, a female lover

Mars: aggression, self-assertion, enterprise, arguments, dominance, contests, competition, battles, physical sports, a male lover

Jupiter: development, expansion, growth, vitality, justice, mentorship, sponsorship, fairness, preservation, good fortune, fulfillment, an authority figure

Saturn: discipline, restriction, constraints, barriers, control, regulation, study, self-improvement, plans, resources, depression, duty, an elder or grandparent

Those who feel confident enough to place the modifiers freely around the circle of the zodiacal trumps, without limiting themselves to the ruling signs of the planets, must take care when placing more than one planetary trump. The aspects defined by their relative positions on the zodiacal circle must reinforce and magnify their combined working so that they assist in the fulfillment of the ritual, or at the very least, do not hinder the ritual. A basic knowledge is needed concerning the conjunction, opposition, square, trine, sextile, and semi-sextile aspects of astrology. The role of the aspects is less important than the role of the planetary trumps selected, but there is value in including the aspects as part of the ritual when two or more planetary modifiers are used.

An aspect is an angle between two planets on the circle of the zodiac by which the zodiac may be divided into equal parts. The angle is measured from the center of the zodiac. Because the trumps of the planetary modifiers are always placed directly over the trumps of the signs, aspects in Tarot magic are always created in round increments of thirty degrees.

It is an old and general rule of thumb in astrology that trine and sextile are good or beneficial aspects, square and opposition are evil or malefic aspects, and conjunction is sometimes good or sometimes evil depending on its contributing factors. Like all old rules of thumb, it should not be accepted without understanding. The square aspect acquired a reputation as evil merely because it is disruptive, yet it is an aspect of great assertion and energy, and this can be successfully applied to useful purposes in Tarot magic, when employed with discretion. The trine aspect, although regarded as good, is so harmonious that it lacks initiating force and may sometimes result in stalemate or inertia unless appropriately used. The semi-sextile is regarded as a weak aspect of little consequence one way or the other. It will do no harm, but where possible, a more energetic aspect should be employed when placing the modifiers on the zodiacal circle.

Opposition: Trumps of the planets on opposite signs in the zodiac, 180° apart or separated by five unoccupied intervening signs, are said to be in opposition. They antagonize and cause the maximum possible tension, resulting in a polarization of their forces. Energy will rebound back and forth between them, resulting in an instability and a frustration of effort. They are like water and oil, refusing to mix even when thrown together, or like two dragons locked in mortal combat, each striving to dominate the other. However, planets in opposition can complement as well as oppose each other, so the effect of this aspect can sometimes be productive.

Trine: Modifier cards set 120° apart on the circle of the zodiac, or separated by three unoccupied intervening signs, are in trine aspect. They are balanced and harmonious, but are lacking in motivational energy. Their combined action is conservative and predictable in its outcome, involving an equality of intercommunication and a shared effort. The Sun and Moon in trine aspect are especially favorable when these modifiers are placed without regard to ruling signs.

Square: Planetary trumps set on the zodiac 90° apart, with two unoccupied intervening signs between them, are said to be in square aspect because they define a right angle, like the corner of a square. The square aspect is capable of generating great amounts of energy through the sudden release of tension. This is a good aspect to move events forward or provoke change. Its power overcomes stagnation, but can be disruptive or revolutionary, and the change it initiates is permanent, or at least significant. It is sometimes called the angle of pain and sorrow. Alan Leo wrote: "The square is probably the only aspect that may be considered as positively evil, although even here good may arise out of the apparent evil" (*Esoteric Astrology*, 80).

Sextile: When modifiers are set on the zodiacal circle at 60° from each other, with one unoccupied intervening sign between them, they are in sextile aspect. The sextile is related to the trine aspect, in that it is also harmonious, but to this is added shared understanding. Planets in this aspect combine their natures together. It is best used in intellectual, esthetic, or artistic situations where a dialogue and a rapport must be maintained. The sextile aspect is more active and potent in causing change than the trine aspect, which is more passive.

Semi-sextile: Placing two planetary modifier trumps on adjacent zodiacal trumps, separated by 30° with no unoccupied intervening signs between them, results in the semi-sextile aspect. It is associated with the trine and sextile. The semi-sextile is a favorable but weak aspect and should generally be avoided where it is possible to form more potent aspects. Its harmonious energy tends to become lost beneath its inertia.

Conjunction: When two modifiers are laid together on the trump of the same sign, they are in conjunction. The separation between them is zero degrees. The planetary trump that is placed on top is dominant over the planetary trump it covers. Its action will guide and control the combined working of the two modifiers. The trumps of two planets in the same sign always act together in unison, whether they are in harmony or there is a dynamic tension between them. The action of one invariably affects the action of the other, so that it is difficult to consider them separately. Sometimes planets in conjunction neutralize each other.

19

MEANINGS OF THE NUMBER CARDS

In the system of Golden Dawn correspondences used throughout this work, each number card of the four suits of the Minor Arcana from the Twos to the Tens receives its own unique title and ten degrees of the zodiac, called a decanate. Each decanate is ruled by a planet. Much of the meaning of the number cards in the Golden Dawn system is derived from the combined planet and sign of its decanate, but meaning also stems from the location of the cards on the Sephiroth and the planets assigned to them on the Tree of Life, from the general influence of the suit element, and from the intrinsic meaning of the numbers themselves. The Aces are regarded as separate and distinct from the other number cards in the Golden Dawn system, and are described as the roots of the powers of the elements.

Whereas the trumps concern forces that transcend the everyday events of mundane human existence, and the court cards represent different types of human nature, the number cards from Two to Ten are ideally suited to express actual happenings in the lives of individual human beings.

The meanings given here are intended only as examples of the infinite uses of the number cards for practical magic. Any purpose you wish to realize will find its representation in the thirty-six suit cards from Two to Ten. The better you understand the number cards, the easier you will find it to select the card, or cards, that accurately expresses your ritual desire. You should look upon these brief meanings as suggestive keys to understanding the number cards, but should not limit your use of the cards solely to the functions listed below. Think about the titles of the cards, along with the decanates and Sephiroth that influence them, and develop your own understanding of what they can accomplish.

Some of the cards have hostile or destructive interpretations. The Tarot is a mirror of the entire world, with all its parts, both helpful and harmful. The evil of the world is reflected in the Tarot, along with the good. Ritual magic is morally neutral—a tool that can be used for both benevolent and malicious purposes. It is possible to employ these negative cards for works of evil magic, but no responsible magician will do so, if only because such malice tends to rebound on those who send it.

Another more productive approach is to use the negative cards to embody the hurtful forces they represent, as a way of neutralizing them. For example, the Three of Swords might be used in a malicious way to cause unhappiness, separation, or disruption. However, it can also be intelligently employed to represent a source of disruption, and by acting on this card with limiting or modifying energies represented by other cards, the source of disruption can be banished or neutralized.

It is also possible to use the power of these negative cards as weapons in honorable ways in the defense of others, or for the punishment of those who have committed harmful or evil acts. This use is fraught with peril, since it is difficult to be sure that punishment sent to others is justified, and there is always the chance that it will rebound on the person who sends it. My recommendation is that you employ the cards with harmful meanings only as a way of representing similar threats, and in this way, contain them.

Two of Wands
Lord of Dominion (Mars in 1–10° Aries, zodiac in Chokmah)
To exert initial influence over others; to express power, authority, dominion.

Three of Wands
Lord of Established Strength (Sun in 11–20° Aries, Saturn in Binah)
To establish existing authority over others; to solidify a dominant position.

Four of Wands
Lord of Perfected Work (Venus in 21–30° Aries, Jupiter in Chesed)
To bring about a settlement or arrangement; to complete an agreement.

Five of Wands
Lord of Strife (Saturn in 1–10° Leo, Mars in Geburah)
To cause quarrels and strife between others; to initiate a conflict.

Six of Wands
Lord of Victory (Jupiter in 11–20° Leo, Sun in Tiphareth)
To gain the benefit of a battle; to obtain success after enduring difficulties.

Seven of Wands
Lord of Valor (Mars in 21–30° Leo, Venus in Netzach)
To generate courage; to confront opposition and overcome it.

Eight of Wands
Lord of Swiftness (Mercury in 1–10° Sagittarius, Mercury in Hod)
To bring about hasty actions or communications; to make things happen at once.

Nine of Wands
Lord of Great Strength (Moon in 11–20° Sagittarius, Moon in Yesod)
To apply steady, unshakable force; to banish weakness, infirmity or sickness.

Ten of Wands

Lord of Oppression (Saturn in 21–30° Sagittarius, four elements in Malkuth)

To exact revenge against an enemy; to apply force for malicious purposes.

Two of Cups

Lord of Love (Venus in 1–10° Cancer, zodiac in Chokmah)

To achieve a happy marriage and a harmonious home; for any pleasure in life.

Three of Cups

Lord of Abundance (Mercury in 11–20° Cancer, Saturn in Binah)

To obtain social pleasure, good hospitality; for a successful party, new clothes, or a feast.

Four of Cups

Lord of Blended Pleasure (Moon in 21–30° Cancer, Jupiter in Chesed)

To extend the enjoyment of luxury or pleasure; to sustain satisfaction.

Five of Cups

Lord of Loss in Pleasure (Mars in 1–10° Scorpio, Mars in Geburah)

To cause disappointment in love; make division between friends.

Six of Cups

Lord of Pleasure (Sun in 11–20° Scorpio, Sun in Tiphareth)

To initiate a period of steady growth; to bring about success.

Seven of Cups

Lord of Illusionary Success (Venus in 21–30° Scorpio, Venus in Netzach)

To cause the illusion of success; to make goals appear deceptively attainable.

Eight of Cups

Lord of Abandoned Success (Saturn in 1-10° Pisces, Mercury in Hod)

To provoke the abandonment of an achievement; the throwing away of a victory.

Nine of Cups

Lord of Material Happiness (Jupiter in 11-20° Pisces, Moon in Yesod)

To achieve complete and perfect satisfaction; to fulfill a wish.

Ten of Cups

Lord of Perfected Success (Mars in 21-30° Pisces, four elements in Malkuth)

To cause sustained good fortune; to ensure lasting success.

Two of Swords

Lord of Peace Restored (Moon in 1-10° Libra, zodiac in Chokmah)

To mend a quarrel; to restore peace or arrange a truce.

Three of Swords

Lord of Sorrow (Saturn in 11-20° Libra, Saturn in Binah)

To cause unhappiness, sorrow, or tears; to make a disruption or separation.

Four of Swords

Lord of Rest from Strife (Jupiter in 21-30° Libra, Jupiter in Chesed)

To bring about a recovery from sickness or worry; to ensure peace after strife.

Five of Swords

Lord of Defeat (Venus in 1-10° Aquarius, Mars in Geburah)

To bring about defeat, failure; to cause loss of authority or position.

Six of Swords

Lord of Earned Success (Mercury in 11–20° Aquarius, Sun in Tiphareth)

To ensure deserved success after labor; to travel safely over water.

Seven of Swords

Lord of Unstable Effort (Moon in 21–30° Aquarius, Venus in Netzach)

To cause someone to quit; to make them cease an effort on the point of victory.

Eight of Swords

Lord of Shortened Force (Jupiter in 1–10° Gemini, Mercury in Hod)

To restrict or imprison another person; to distract them with petty details.

Nine of Swords

Lord of Despair and Cruelty (Mars in 11–20° Gemini, Moon in Yesod)

To cause despair, suffering, or misery; to make oppression, persecution.

Ten of Swords

Lord of Ruin (Sun in 21–30° Gemini, four elements in Malkuth)

To bring about disruption of work; to cause the final defeat of an enemy.

Two of Pentacles

Lord of Harmonious Change (Jupiter in 1–10° Capricorn, zodiac in Chokmah)

To cause a pleasant change of place or experience; to induce others to visit you.

Three of Pentacles

Lord of Material Works (Mars in 11–20° Capricorn, Saturn in Binah)

To find a job; to close a business deal or succeed in a transaction.

Four of Pentacles
Lord of Earthly Power (Sun in 21–30° Capricorn, Jupiter in Chesed)
To get a gift or acquire money; to gain valuable influence.

Five of Pentacles
Lord of Material Trouble (Mercury in 1–10° Taurus, Mars in Geburah)
To cause the loss of a job; to make money troubles, anxiety over financial situation.

Six of Pentacles
Lord of Material Success (Moon in 11–20° Taurus, Sun in Tiphareth)
To cause prosperity in business; to gain success in material matters.

Seven of Pentacles
Lord of Success Unfulfilled (Saturn in 21–30° Taurus, Venus in Netzach)
To make work or an investment unprofitable; to cause little gain for much labor.

Eight of Pentacles
Lord of Prudence (Sun in 1–10° Virgo, Mercury in Hod)
To induce prudence in the handling of money; to find hidden wealth or objects.

Nine of Pentacles
Lord of Material Gain (Venus in 11–20° Virgo, Moon in Yesod)
To increase goods or possessions; to inherit money or valuables.

Ten of Pentacles
Lord of Wealth (Mercury in 21–30° Virgo, Four elements in Malkuth)
To attain desired wealth; to achieve success in money transactions.

20

Using Realizers
and Modifiers

The number cards apart from the Aces may be called *realizers* because they represent the fulfillment of the ritual desire, which is the purpose for which the ritual has been conducted. When a single number card is placed on the triangle of realization, it expresses the achievement of a simple purpose. Many useful rituals can be worked with only a lone realizer on the triangle. However, to more completely express a fulfillment that takes place in several stages, or has several parts, it is necessary to use more than one number card.

Rituals often have as their focus a human being, who is represented on the triangle by a significator. It is possible to work rituals using only a lone significator on the triangle, but all of the definition for the ritual purpose must then come from the intention of the magician, aided by whichever planetary modifiers are used. The significator card on the triangle characterizes by its esoteric associations the person at whom the ritual is aimed, and when it is unaccompanied by realizers the nature of the fulfillment must be held dynamically in the mind of the magician.

It is often more effective to combine a significator on the triangle with one or more realizers. The number cards act to define and channel the purpose of the ritual; the court card acts to identify the individual at whom the ritual is directed. By using more than a single number card on the triangle, the unfolding of a complex purpose is accurately defined; by joining the realizers with a significator, this complex purpose is precisely focused on its living target.

The realizers are placed beneath the significator on the triangle in a stack of cards so that they express in sequence from the top to the bottom of the stack, first the person who is the focus of the ritual, and then the various parts of its fulfillment. The first card on top of the realizer stack occupies the present moment, and successive cards beneath it express actions realized in the future. The final card on the bottom of the stack is the final outcome sought by the ritual.

In Tarot magic, as in life, there can be too much of a good thing. Just as it is usually unwise to use all seven planetary modifiers at once, so also is it a bad practice to employ a large number of realizers. By trying to define the outcome of the ritual too narrowly, its freedom of working will be choked and inhibited. Magic needs a little wiggle room in which to fulfill itself. The number cards that realize the ritual should express only the purpose itself, not rigorously plot out its unfolding. From one to three number cards works best. More may be used, but as they are multiplied on the triangle, the likelihood of a successful ritual goes down. Strive for clarity and simplicity when constructing rituals, and concentrate on the desire fulfilled, not the manner of its fulfillment.

When working with a single realizer on the triangle, it is often useful to place on the circle the planetary modifier that corresponds with the planet in the decanate of that number card. This creates a potent resonance between the triangle and the circle. For example, if you performed a ritual to acquire money from a certain individual, you would put on the triangle of realization the significator best suited to represent that person, and beneath it the Four of Pentacles, the Lord of Earthly Power. The Four of Pentacles is linked in the Golden Dawn system with the second decanate of Capricorn, which is ruled by the astrological planet the Sun. The planet the Sun is in the Golden Dawn correspondences linked with the trump the Sun. Therefore you would place the trump the Sun on top of its ruling sign Leo, which is occupied in the zodiacal circle by Strength. This would create a resonance between the zodiac trump Strength, the planetary trump the Sun, and the number card the Four of Pentacles.

In more complex rituals, when two or three realizers are used on the triangle, the planetary modifier of each may be placed on its ruling sign in the circle. Care should be taken where possible not to create aspects between the planetary trumps on the circle that are unfavorable to the achievement of the ritual purpose. In general, the choice of the modifiers is more important than the aspects they define, but if you can avoid a disharmonious aspect, it is sensible to do so. Aspects can be manipulated because five of the seven planets rule two signs. Whether a modifier is placed on the sign it rules in the solar or lunar sect has less influence on the outcome of the ritual than the aspects it forms, so consideration of aspects should be given precedence. By intelligently choosing which sign will receive the planetary trump, unfortunate aspects can often be avoided.

Square aspects, in which two modifiers are placed at 90° from each other on the circle, with two empty signs between them, are generally not helpful, unless you deliberately seek to sow discord. Similarly, Opposition should be avoided between two modifiers unless you want to create tension. By contrast, trine aspects, in which two modifiers are placed at 120° from each other with three empty signs between them, result in the energies of the two planets working in harmony, as do sextile aspects, in which modifiers are placed at 60° from each other with one empty sign between them. These are the most important of the aspects. It may happen that two number cards used on the triangle have the same planet ruling their decanates. The single planetary modifier will then serve to represent both of them, and the harmony of their working will be perfect.

Use of planetary modifiers is not limited to the planets ruling the decanates of the number cards on the triangle, nor must the modifiers be located solely on the signs in the zodiacal circle they rule, although this is generally the easiest method of ensuring that the modifiers will be appropriate to the purpose of the ritual, and

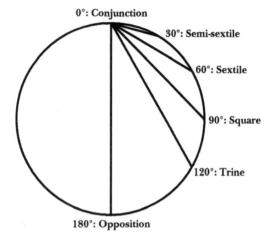

Aspects on the Zodiacal Circle

will aid in its fulfillment. It is a mechanical system of placement that can be relied upon to yield good results, without the need to weigh and balance the various forces involved, but it is not mandatory.

If you are confident that you fully understand the meanings of the planets in the zodiac signs, any modifier may be used on the circle with any number card, or cards, in the triangle. The different occult potentials that may be generated in this way are from a practical standpoint infinite. Some will help the ritual purpose and others will harm it, so it is necessary to choose wisely.

For example, suppose you wished to unite an older man and a younger woman in a romantic relationship. You would pick for the significator of the man the King that best expressed his personality, and for the young woman would choose the most appropriate Page. To express the realization of the purpose, a loving union, the number card the Two of Cups, titled the Lord of Love, would be appropriate. These three cards would be stacked on the triangle, the King on top, the Page below, and the Two of Cups on the bottom of the stack to represent the fulfillment of the purpose.

The planet Venus rules the first decanate of Cancer, which is the decanate given to the Two of Cups. The planetary modifier of Venus is the Empress, which seems a very appropriate choice for this ritual. This might be placed on either of the two signs ruled by Venus, which are Taurus and Libra, were it to be located according to the mechanical method already described. However, a more creative use of the modifier of the planet Venus, the trump the Empress, would be to locate it upon the sign of Aries, which is occupied by the zodiacal trump the Emperor. The sign Aries is ruled by the planet Mars, and Venus and Mars are natural lovers, as are the Empress and the Emperor.

The complexity that may be achieved in the interplay of occult forces between the realizers, the modifiers, and the zodiacal trumps allows a cornucopia of choices. Do not be intimidated by it if you are a beginner and have little understanding of astrology. Start your practice of Tarot rituals without using any planetary modifiers on the circle. When you gain confidence that you understand the basics, use modifiers that match the ruling planets of the decanates of the number cards on the triangle, and place the modifiers on the signs their planets rule in the zodiac. This will prevent you from obstructing the fulfillment of the ritual.

It is best to begin with only a single realizer on the triangle to stand for your purpose, or a significator and a realizer to represent the person the ritual is about and the fulfillment you seek. A single significator and a single realizer on the triangle, with a single modifier on the circle that is linked to the realizer by the ruling planet of its decanate, make a conflict of energies almost impossible. After you gain confidence in your rituals, you can increase the realizers to a maximum of three, and the corresponding modifiers to three. It is not essential to have a planetary modifier for each realizer card, but it results in a fertile balance.

21

SUMMARY OF
ESSENTIALS

The cards in a ritual that allow you to define its purpose are the significators, the modifiers, and the realizers.

Significators are the sixteen court cards that represent you, any person for whom you may be serving as an agent, or any human being who is the focus of the ritual. Your own significator is always placed on the altar of the four Aces, at the center of the zodiacal circle, which esoterically is the center of the universe during the ritual. The significator of a person for whom you act as the agent is placed just beneath your own significator card. The significator of a person you wish the ritual to act on is placed upon the triangle of realization.

If you act as agent for more than one person simultaneously, the significators of each person are placed beneath your own card. If the ritual is directed at more than one person, the significators of those who are the targets of the ritual are placed together on the triangle. It is usually more effective to act as agent for only a single individual, and to direct the energies of the ritual at no more than one person. However, at times it may become necessary to use a greater number of significators. For example, if you were to act as agent for a mother and child together against the threat of the estranged father, the significators of the mother and child would be placed beneath your own significator card on the elemental altar, and the significator of the father would occupy the triangle.

When two or more significators are used in a ritual, it may not always be possible to select the ideal court card to serve as a significator for an individual, if the best card is already in use. You should choose the most appropriate court card for the significator of your subject or the person for whom you act as agent from among the remaining available court cards. Your own significator is always selected first as the ideal court card to represent you, and does not change from ritual to ritual.

Planetary modifiers are the seven trumps linked to the traditional planets of astrology. They are potent active forces that unbalance the harmony of the ritual circle, allowing it to fill more easily with the energies associated with the modifier, or modifiers, used. Modifiers color the circle with their natures. When placed over the trumps of the signs they rule, their energies act freely and with force. When a modifier is placed on a sign it does not rule, its action will depend on the interplay between the planet and the sign. In general, modifiers not on their ruling signs function less powerfully than modifiers on their ruling signs.

The action of any modifier is strongest if it is used alone. Placed on the lunar sect, its working will tend to be more subtle or secret, less material and less overt. Placed on the solar sect, the action of a modifier will tend to be active, more aggressive, obvious, and emphatic. Use of two or more modifiers blends the qualities of the planets they represent. The combined action of two or more modifiers is strengthened by aspects in harmony with the ritual purpose, but weakened by discordant aspects.

Realizers are the number cards of the suits from Two to Ten that correspond with the Sephiroth on the Tree of Life from Chokmah to Malkuth. Each takes its identity from the elemental association of its suit, the nature and associations of the Sephirah to which it belongs, its decanate and the ruling planet of that decanate in the Golden Dawn system of correspondences, and the inherent significance of its own number. The purpose of the ritual may be embodied in only a single realizer, or in a series of number cards that are stacked one above the other on the triangle of realization. Stacked cards tell a kind of narrative that expresses symbolically the desired fulfillment of the ritual purpose.

The number card on the top of a realizer stack represents desired change applied to the present situation. Each successive card beneath it is the next stage in the progress of the realization of the ritual. The final number card in the stack is the final stage of fulfillment of the purpose for which the ritual is worked. None of the realizer cards represent the past. The past does not play a part in expressing the fulfillment of the magical desire, because that desire is wholly in the future. In Tarot divination, the cards of a layout may express the past, present, and future, but in Tarot magic they express only the present and future.

When a significator is used on the triangle in combination with realizers, it should be placed on top of the realizer stack. It is separate from the timeline of events expressed by the realizer stack and encompasses the entire timeline, as would be expected since any human life naturally contains many events. By placing it on top, it is easier to form a bond between your own significator on the altar, and the significator on the triangle of the person at whom the ritual is directed.

The cards that are to form the structure of the ritual are selected before beginning. The ritual should be completely planned out and understood before it is undertaken so that the cards may be laid with confidence and no hesitation. All cards are prepared face up, and are laid in the ritual face up. Separate them into stacks in their correct sequence—the Aces of the altar, the trumps of the zodiacal circle, the trumps of any planetary modifiers that you intend to use, the trumps of the triangle of realization, and the number card or cards that are to be placed on the triangle.

Your own significator and the significators of those for whom you act as agent, if this is part of the ritual, and the person or persons at whom the ritual is directed, should be placed on the working surface separately so they can be located without delay. Cards should always be laid down individually, but may be prepared in groups. For example, if you act as the agent for two people, you can put their two significator cards together in readiness, but you should place them on the altar individually, one atop the other, before placing your own significator. Generally speaking, the last card placed in a ritual layout will be the significator on the triangle, representing the person at whom the ritual is directed; or, if there is no significator used on the triangle, the last card will be the uppermost realizer.

You can sit anywhere, facing any direction, and lay the cards out on any surface, but for ease of orientation it is best to sit facing east and to lay the cards out in front of yourself on a table. In the illustrations of the altar and the circle shown in this book, the perspective is from the south looking north. This was done because this is the usual way maps are presented, with the east on the right side. When you work a ritual, the zodiacal trump of the Emperor will always be in the east, but you can sit on any side of the circle you choose. The location of the triangle, whether east, south, west, or north, will depend on the nature of the ritual purpose, whether it is airy, fiery, watery, or earthy.

Gathering up the cards at the end of the ritual signifies its end. It is best to gather the cards up individually in the reverse order to which they were laid out. If you make a mistake gathering up the cards it is not fatal to the ritual fulfillment. Shuffling the cards wipes them clean of their ritual associations, so that they may be used again to represent other individuals, and other ritual purposes. There is no danger that a specific meaning will be burned into a card permanently. Just as is true in Tarot divination, when the cards are shuffled in Tarot magic, they are randomized and in this way returned to a chaotic state. Since there are only seventy-eight Tarot cards, and an infinite possible number of meanings in the world, it is necessary that each card be able to express more than a single meaning, both in divination and in ritual. Shuffling the cards is what allows them to do so.

22

RITUAL OF UNION

It is possible to unite psychically with another person on a very deep level using the Tarot cards, if you know the time and place of that person's birth, or possess an astrological birth chart of the person. The chart will show the signs of the zodiac on which the seven planets fall at the time of birth. If only the date and place of birth are known, an astrologer can construct a chart that will supply this information. The day of birth will usually be precise enough to place the planets accurately. Because Tarot magic does not concern itself with individual degrees of the zodiac, but only with the twelve signs, it is enough if each planet is located within its sign, and basing a chart on the day of birth will do that most of the time since the planets, even the Moon, move slowly through the signs (the Moon spends over two days in each sign). If you can obtain the exact hour and minute of birth, so much the better.

This ritual of union is an exception to the general rule that all seven planetary modifiers should not be used together on the circle. It is usually the case that the greater the number of modifiers, the weaker their action, but when employed in the pattern of a horoscope they work together to define the person represented by the horoscope. A birth chart is like a fingerprint in the stars. It captures a snapshot of the heavens from the perspective of a particular place and a specific moment in time. The chart can only be represented in the ritual layout in a simplified form, but it is still an intimate expression of the individual for whom it was cast.

Uses for this ritual include the projection of thoughts or ideas into the mind of the individual identified by the horoscope layout; the psychic perception of that person's thoughts, emotions, or intentions; the projection into the mind of the person of impulses to perform specific actions; the domination of the will of the other person, should this ever be necessary for your defense or the protection of others; the projection of specific dream images or visions. It is a more active, forceful, dominant form of union than the method mentioned earlier, in which the magician places his or her significator on the altar in the ritual circle, with the significator of another individual beneath it.

For a practical example, I will assume that we wish to form a bridge of communication with the spirit of Samuel L. MacGregor Mathers, the leader of the Golden Dawn. It is possible to form links with those who have died, or at least with spiritual intelligences who have assumed their identities and personalities and assert themselves to be the souls of those who once were alive. Whether these are the actual souls of the dead is a philosophical question difficult to resolve. Mathers's birth chart has the Moon in Aries, Saturn in Taurus, Mars in Leo, Mercury in Sagittarius, Jupiter in Sagittarius, the Sun in Capricorn, and Venus in Aquarius.

Form the elemental altar using the four Aces in the manner already described, so that the interlaced bases of the cards express a spiral motion. Upon the center of this altar, lay your own significator in an upright attitude from your perspective. If it can be done conveniently, it is best to sit facing the east.

Imagine yourself standing upon the significator as though on a colorful rug in the middle of the altar dais, facing east with your arms spread so that your body forms a cross.

Touch the tip of your right index finger to your significator and say the words:

"The heart of the four."

Touch in succession the Ace of Swords, Ace of Cups, Ace of Pentacles, and Ace of Wands, so that your finger describes a cross above the altar. As you touch the cards, say:

"The Sword before me, the Cup behind me, the Pentacle on my left hand, the Wand on my right hand."

As you touch each Ace, visualize in the astral space the symbol of its suit materialize in the air above the end of its card-rug. Each symbol flickers and shines with golden radiance.

Again, touch your significator with your right fingertip and say the words:

"The center of the universe."

Visualize a cross of golden beams extending itself outward in the four directions from your heart center as you stand on the altar with your arms spread wide. Each beam pierces the symbol of its suit. Mentally lower your arms and contemplate this cross for several moments, then allow it to fade from your imagination.

Lay out the circle of the zodiacal trumps in the usual way, beginning in the east with the Emperor on Aries and proceeding clockwise around the circle to the trump the Moon on Pisces. If you are sitting in the west facing east, Aries will be at the top of the circle from your perspective.

With the tip of your right index finger, touch again your significator on the altar. Visualize yourself standing on the altar facing east, and imagine that you touch your chest with your hand over your heart center as you speak these words:

"The All in One."

Touch each card of the circle in turn with your right index finger, beginning with the Emperor and proceeding clockwise. Pause for a moment after touching each card to allow yourself to become fully aware of it. As you touch each trump, speak its name:

**"The Emperor, the Hierophant, the Lovers,
the Chariot, Strength, the Hermit, Justice, Death,
Temperance, the Devil, the Star, the Moon."**

At the same time, visualize yourself on the astral level pointing in turn with your right hand at the glowing rectangles of light that float above each zodiacal trump while slowly turning clockwise on your own axis. As you utter each name, mentally project the symbol of its sign into the rectangle in glowing golden light. Take the time to see each symbol clearly before moving on to the next trump.

Touch a second time the trump the Emperor to close the circle, and speak the words:

"The circle is complete."

Touch the significator again and at the same time imagine that you touch your chest over your heart with your right hand as you stand in your astral body on the altar. Speak the words:

"The One in All."

Imagine a ring of golden light expanding from your heart center through the air to link all twelve signs of the zodiac in their rectangles above the rugs of the trumps.

While concentrating on the face of the person with whom you wish to unite your mind, lay all seven planetary modifiers on the circle, beginning with the Emperor in Aries if any planet in the person's birth chart falls on that sign, and proceeding clockwise. The heads of the modifiers point outward, in the same orientation as the trumps of the circle they cover. Planets seldom fall directly on the middle of signs in astrological charts, but the planetary modifiers are always placed directly over the trumps of the signs. If two planets fall on the same sign, both modifiers are placed on top of that zodiacal trump. The circle will resonate strongly with the identifying energies of the person you seek to reach.

When all seven planetary modifiers have been laid on the zodiacal circle, touch each with your right index finger in the order in which they were laid out, moving clockwise around the circle from Aries or the first sign that receives a modifier. If two modifiers lie one on top of the other in a sign, as is the case for Mathers in the sign Sagittarius, tap twice, the first tap for the modifier on top and the second tap for the modifier beneath. It does not greatly matter which planet is put on top when two or more modifiers occupy the same zodiacal trump, since they are treated as being of equal importance. As a general rule, place the most favorable planet on top.

As each modifier is tapped with the right fingertip clockwise around the reflected zodiacal circle, its name is spoken. Since two modifiers occupy the place of Temperance (Sagittarius) in Mathers's chart, it is tapped twice, but it is not necessary to physically touch the lower modifier that is covered by the modifier above it:

"The High Priestess, the World, the Tower, the Magician, the Wheel, the Sun, the Empress."

As you speak the name of each modifier, imagine yourself standing on the astral version of the altar, and point at the rectangle of light above the zodiacal trump that modifier occupies. Mentally project the symbol of the planet of the modifier into the rectangle, so that the symbol of the planet floats above the symbol of the sign. When two or more modifiers fall on a single sign, visualize both symbols of the planets side by side above the symbol of the sign in the rectangle of light.

Build the triangle of realization in the manner already described on the western side of the circle so that the triangle points toward the west. If you are seated in the west facing east, the triangle will point toward you. The west is the appropriate quarter for the location of the triangle in the ritual of union because the west is the quarter of elemental Water in the system of the Golden Dawn, and Water is the element associated with psychic activity.

Take up the final card of the ritual, which is the significator of the person with whom you seek union. In the case of Mathers, the best choice would be the King of Swords. Mathers loved the military and was a boxer and fencer. He had a keen intellect and projected his personality through his words. He was by nature dominant and combative. The King of Cups might also be a reasonable choice, given Mathers's psychic abilities and his tendency to become abstracted and daydream, but we will use the King of Swords. If your own significator happens to be the same as that chosen for your subject, you must use the next most appropriate court card as the significator for your subject.

Lay the significator of the person you are trying to contact on the triangle of realization so that it rests on the middle of the triangle and points away from the center of the circle, in the same orientation as the Fool. If you are seated in the west facing east, and the triangle is in the west, this court card will be upside down from your own perspective, but this does not matter. The significator on the triangle is always oriented with reference to the center of the circle, which is its down or ground.

The illustration shows the modifiers on the zodiacal trumps, with the triangle in the west. Note that your significator on the altar is upright from your own perspective if you were physically sitting on the western side of the circle, facing east. Remember that the orientation of your own significator depends on where you sit, but that the orientation of the other cards is always to the center of the circle, with the exception of the three elemental trumps, which are orientated to the center of the triangle.

Visualize yourself standing on the dais of the astral altar, facing the triangle in the west.

Touch with your right fingertip the three trumps of the triangle in turn counterclockwise around the triangle, saying their names:

"The Fool, the Hanged Man, Judgement."

NORTH

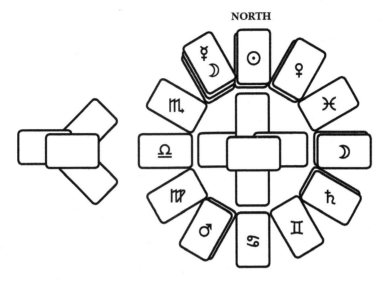

Ritual of Union Layout

Again, touch the Fool to close the triangle. Say the words:

"The triangle is prepared."

As you stand in your imagination in the center of the astral circle of the ritual place speaking these words, visualize an upright triangle of white light form itself on the air about a foot above the three supine, interwoven elemental trumps. The left side forms first, then the base, and finally the right side. It is the same height as the rectangles of light that float about the rugs of the trumps in the astral circle.

Touch your own significator on the altar with your right index finger, saying:

"The purpose is willed."

Concentrate your mind strongly on the other person so that your imagination is filled with that person's identity. Hold in your awareness the person's face. Mentally voice the name of that person. Try to feel that person close to you, aware of your presence.

Charge the circle with the energy of your intention. On the astral level, imagine the force of your will forming a swirling vortex of translucent light similar to a whirlwind that glows on the air within the circle and has its focus on your astral body. The whirlwind turns in a sunwise, or clockwise, direction.

Touch with your right index finger the significator of the other person on the triangle, saying:

"The purpose is fulfilled."

At once release your will to be united with the other person. Direct it with your right hand and arm as though casting forth a glowing lance of white fire from your heart center through the center of the triangle of golden light that floats upon the air above the raised dais of the three elemental trumps. Feel yourself snatch the fiery lance of your will out of your heart center and fling it through the center of the triangle. Visualize the upright astral triangle filling with bright radiance.

Once more touch with your index finger your own significator in the center of the zodiacal circle, saying:

"The way is open."

Visualize on the astral level a returning bolt of light emerge from the upright triangle and flash into your heart center. It is immediately reflected and darts forth back to the triangle. This pulse of light flies back and forth faster and faster for several seconds until it forms a solid beam of white light between your chest and the upright triangle. Not only imagine seeing this reciprocal pulse, but also feel it in your astral body.

An esoteric link has been formed through the opened portal of the Fool between your unconscious mind and the unconscious mind of the other person, or in the case of our example, the awareness of the spirit of MacGregor Mathers. The bridge is the highest spiritual level, which is equivalent to Kether on the Tree of Life. As long as you do not disturb the layout, the portal will remain open.

Contemplate the significator on the triangle with your mind relaxed and receptive. You will find it easy to project your thoughts to that person, or to project with your will any actions you wish that person to perform. Your level of success will depend on your skill in projecting your will and your ability to relax your mind so that your own thoughts do not interfere with your intentions. If you are passively psychic, you will find that you can sense the mood and intentions of the person in the triangle, and perhaps even hear their thoughts if your gift is great. Always you will feel yourself very close to the other person.

When you are finished interacting with your subject, take up the cards one by one in the reverse order to the way they were laid out and shuffle them. Taking up the cards breaks the reciprocating ray between the two significators and closes the portal. Shuffling removes the associations of the ritual from the cards and cleanses them for their next ritual use.

23

BANISHING RITUAL

The Banishing Ritual may be done daily as a way of becoming familiar with the symbolic structures of Tarot magic, and with the manipulation of the esoteric forces of the cards. It serves to cleanse the astral place of working and to dispel any unbalanced elemental energies. It is also an excellent way to cleanse a physical space such as a room, or a structure such as a house, or even an open space such as a field. Construction of the triangle of realization is not required for this ritual. Note that in the illustration, the significator on the altar has been oriented to be upright from your point of view when you are seated on the western side of the circle, facing the east.

Start with a clean, flat surface that represents in a symbolic sense the unlimited surface of the astral plane. Erect the elemental altar of the four Aces in the manner already described. The interwoven Aces create a spiral of force that descends downward in a clockwise turning, viewed from the top. Think of them as the blades of a propeller that turns clockwise. The spiral forms automatically when the altar is erected, and energizes the center of the altar. Lay your significator on top of the cross of Aces so that it is upright from your perspective and centered over the altar. It will be elevated slightly above the level of the table—the effect is more noticeable when you use small, stiff cards, which have more tilt when interlaced. The spiral created by the turning of the Aces has its focus on the center of your significator.

Touch your right index finger to the center of your significator. As you do so, visualize yourself standing on the raised dais of the astral altar facing east with your arms spread wide so that your body forms a cross. Say the words:

"The heart of the four."

In turn, touch the Ace of Swords, Ace of Cups, Ace of Pentacles, and Ace of Wands, so that your finger draws a cross in the air above the altar. As you touch the Aces, say:

"The Sword before me, the Cup behind me, the Pentacle on my left hand, the Wand on my right hand."

As you speak the name of each suit symbol, it appears on the astral level floating upright on the air above the head of its card. A glowing sword floats vertically with its point upward upon the air of the east in front of you. Behind you floats a glowing cup upon the air in the west. At your left in the north floats a glowing pentacle. At your right side in the south, a glowing wand floats.

Touch once again your significator, and say:

"The center of the universe."

Visualize four beams of golden light extending outward from your heart center to pierce the four symbols of the suits. The beams of this cross of light continue infinitely into the distance. Lower your arms as you stand upon the altar and contemplate the cross for several moments, then allow it to fade from your imagination.

Lay out the trumps of the zodiacal circle around the elemental altar, beginning with the Emperor in the place of Aries in the east, and proceeding clockwise.

Touch your right index finger to your significator on the altar, and imagine that you touch your right hand to your heart center as you stand in the astral place of working. Say the words:

"The All in One."

Tap each trump in turn lightly with your right index finger, beginning with the Emperor in the east and proceeding clockwise around the circle. As you touch each card, speak its name:

"The Emperor, the Hierophant, the Lovers,
the Chariot, Strength, the Hermit, Justice, Death,
Temperance, the Devil, the Star, the Moon."

Imagine yourself standing upon the astral altar within a circle of twelve rectangles of glowing light that float in the air above the rugs of the zodiacal trumps like empty doorways. As you utter the name of each trump, point with your extended index finger at its rectangle and see its sign of the zodiac appear within the rectangle in golden light.

Again touch the trump the Emperor to close the circle. Speak the words:

"The circle is complete."

Touch your significator with the tip of your index finger, and imagine that you touch your chest with your right hand as you stand facing the east upon the astral altar of the ritual place. Say the words:

"The One in All."

A circle of golden light expands outward from your heart center to the twelve rectangles and floats upon the air of the ritual place above the zodiac trumps, linking with its band all twelve signs of the zodiac.

Lay the Ten of Swords just to the east of the Emperor so that the head of the card points eastward, and its base touches the head of the Emperor. Lay the Ten of Wands in the south so that its head points southward and its base touches the top of the Chariot. Lay the Ten of Cups in the west so that its head points westward and its base touches the head of Justice. Lay the Ten of Pentacles in the

NORTH

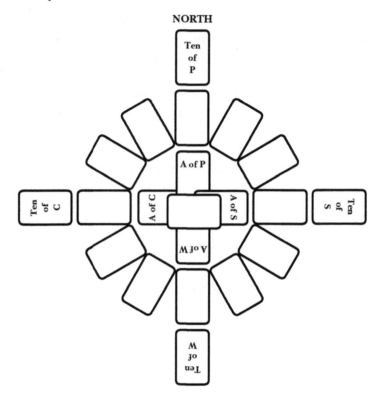

Banishing Ritual Layout

north so that its head points northward and its base touches the head of the Devil. If the Tens happen to shift away from the trumps of the circle during the ritual, do not worry about it, but continue to conceive them as touching in the astral place.

Tap your right index finger to the Ten of Swords and say:

"By the Sword of Air, I banish the kingdom of the east."

Tap your finger to the Ten of Wands and say:

"By the Wand of Fire, I banish the kingdom of the south."

Tap your finger to the Ten of Cups and say:

"By the Cup of Water, I banish the kingdom of the west."

Tap your finger to the Ten of Pentacles and say:

"By the Pentacle of Earth, I banish the kingdom of the north."

As you touch the card of each direction, visualize on the astral level the glowing symbol of the suit that floats above the head of its Ace on the altar descending downward into the card, and a similar but much larger symbol of the suit ascending out of the rug of the Ten that lies beyond the circle. The outer symbol is gigantic and towers above your head.

There is a link between the Ace and the Ten of each suit that acts as a natural portal, which is how the symbolic weapon of the suit can move through the circle without breaking it. Kether and Malkuth are connected, as are the numbers one (01) and ten (10). Together, they represent the most spiritual source of the element and its most material expression.

While holding in your mind the four large elemental weapons that float upright on the air beyond the circle, speak the words:

"By the power of the four, this place is cleansed."

Remain within the astral circle for several minutes and contemplate its atmosphere, which should feel serene yet energized, as though awaiting transformation. Allow yourself to become aware of the physical place where you laid out the cards as you continue to stand within the circle. See both the astral place of working, and the physical space around your physical body at the same time, interpenetrating each other. Expand from the heart center of your astral body a cleansing radiance, so that the physical place in which you have worked the ritual glows with subtle light. Visualize the four elemental weapons floating in the corners of the physical room where you are seated.

Gather up the cards one by one in the reverse order to the way they were laid out, first the four Tens, then the zodiacal circle, then the significator, and lastly the four Aces of the altar. Shuffle them. Shuffling the cards removes the associations specific to any single ritual, so that they can be used for other purposes.

24

Business Ritual

It would be impossible in this small book to give detailed instructions for every ritual that might be worked using Tarot magic. The number of uses to which this system of magic may be put is infinite, and so are the variations of ritual that reflect those purposes. What can be done is to show, through a detailed example, the general ritual procedure applied to a specific practical purpose. The details of the layout will change, depending on the purpose.

Everyone wants success in his or her business or career. Sometimes the difference between success and failure is as slight as gaining an important contract or assignment. In magic, it is best to focus on the attainment of specific goals, rather than attempt to achieve something as nebulous as success in general. The rule of thumb is to work toward specific ends, but to allow magic to find its own way. If you try to dictate during rituals the exact manner in which your desire will be fulfilled, you will strangle and frustrate its fulfillment. Be exact about what you want, but be open and receptive as to how it is gained.

In our example, Mary, a freelance artist in her thirties, seeks to be given a contract by a major publisher to illustrate a soon-to-be-published children's book, which she hopes will become a best-seller and ensure her future work as a book illustrator. Whether she gets the job depends on the recommendation of a senior editor at the publishing house. Mary has already submitted samples of her work based on the manuscript, and is awaiting a decision from the publisher.

She has already selected the Queen of Wands as her own significator. The senior editor in charge of book illustrations at the publishing house is a man in his sixties. Mary knows little of his background, having only talked to him a few times over the phone and exchanged several e-mails with him, but she knows that he is artistic and well-educated, quiet-spoken and cheerful. For his significator she selects the King of Cups.

She breaks down her ritual purpose into three stages, to correspond with three realizer cards. The first is the awarding to her of the contract to illustrate the book. The second is her completion of the assignment. The third is the critical acclaim and popular success that follows the publication of the book. Her purpose is not just to get the contract, but to achieve success in her career as a consequence of getting the contract. In planning a ritual, it is wise to spend some time thinking about its ultimate purpose. In Mary's case, it is not just to get a job, but to get a job that does her career some good.

For the first stage, the beginning of the fulfillment of her purpose, she picks the Three of Pentacles, which bears the title Lord of Material Works. It is of the nature of Mars acting in the second decanate of Capricorn, and also of Saturn modified by the influence of Binah. Pentacles is the suit of elemental Earth, and relates to material realization and manifest actions. Both Mars and Capricorn are strongly masculine, so there is much virile energy in this card. Its action will be overt and practical. Saturn is a cold and distant planet relating to restriction and discipline, but its aridity is softened by its action in the sphere of Binah, the great cosmic womb of creation. Saturn acting through Binah suggests the controlled and calculated investment of resources.

The second stage, concerning the actual work of illustration that she will do, is represented by the Four of Wands, which bears the title Lord of Perfected Work. Its nature is Venus ruling the final decanate of Aries, and also Jupiter acting in the sphere of Chesed. Wands is the suit of elemental Fire and relates to the action of the will, the determination to achieve a goal. Venus in Aries suggests a productive union. Aries is creatively virile, and Venus both fertile and receptive. Their union will bring forth an issue. Jupiter in Chesed shows the happiest of planets in the most benevolent of Sephiroth, both productive influences.

The final stage in the realization of the ritual purpose is represented by the Six of Cups, which bears the title Lord of Pleasure. This card is a good choice for initiating a period of steady growth and success. It is the Sun ruling the second decanate of Scorpio, and also the Sun in Tiphareth. The Sun in Scorpio indicates both heat and penetration. Scorpio concerns the critical phases of transformation in life, resulting in a kind of rebirth. The Sun is the life principle of wholeness and self-integration. Its action in this card is uncommonly strong because it not only rules the decanate of the card, but the Sephiroth where the card resides on the Tree. Tiphareth is the center of the Tree, the sphere of complete balance and harmony. The pleasure of this card is the pleasure of desire realized. Crowley called this card "one of the best in the pack" (*The Book of Thoth*, 182).

These are not the only three cards that might have been selected as realizers of the ritual purpose. Different choices would produce different shades of effect. Some choices would be more appropriate than others, but only the individual who plans the ritual can make the final decision about how effective the selected cards will be in achieving the desired end of the work.

The three planetary modifiers naturally linked to these cards through the decanates of their signs are the Tower (Mars), the Empress (Venus), and the Sun (Sun). The Tower corresponds with Mars, and Mars rules the second decanate of Capricorn, which is given to the Three of Pentacles. The Empress is associated with Venus, and Venus rules the last decanate of Aries, which is given to the Four of Wands. The trump the Sun is associated with the planet the Sun, ruler of the second decanate of Scorpio, which is given to the Six of Cups.

The easiest way to place modifiers is on their own ruling signs. The trump the Sun, linked with the planet the Sun, is located on the zodiacal trump Strength in the sign Leo. There is no need to make a choice since the planet the Sun only rules one sign. The Empress, linked with Venus, may be placed on either Taurus (Hierophant) or Libra (Justice), both signs ruled by the planet Venus. The Tower, linked with Mars, may be placed on either Aries (Emperor) or Scorpio (Death), both signs ruled by the planet Mars.

In the illustration, the modifier the Empress (Venus) has been put on the sign Libra and the zodiacal trump Justice, which is in the solar sect. The modifier the Tower (Mars) has been put on the sign Aries and the zodiacal trump the Emperor, in the lunar sect. The aspect between the modifier trump the Sun and the modifier trump the Empress is the benign sextile aspect. The aspect between the modifier the Sun and the modifier the Tower is the harmonious trine aspect. The Empress and the Tower are in an opposition aspect to each other, which creates a dynamic tension, not necessarily a bad thing because it generates energy.

Had the modifier the Tower (Mars) been placed on its other ruled sign, Scorpio, a square aspect would have been created with the modifier the Sun. Similarly, had the modifier the Empress (Venus) been located on its other ruled sign Taurus, a square aspect would also have been formed with the modifier the Sun. In general, square aspects are to be avoided where possible when rituals are worked for productive, harmonious purposes. In the case of a ritual deliberately constructed to cause discord or conflict for a necessary and justifiable purpose, square aspects might be desirable, but in our example we will avoid them.

The primary meaning of the zodiacal trump Death (Scorpio) is transformation. In spite of its somewhat sinister appearance, it has great active power and should not be avoided when placing the planetary modifiers. This is also true of the other trump of the circle that superficially appears to have an evil connotation, the Devil (Capricorn). Both cards express considerable force that can be used in rituals with excellent results. In our example, the Tower is put on the Emperor rather than on Death to avoid a square aspect, not to avoid the Death trump.

There is one more thing to determine—the location for the triangle of realization. This requires some thought. Should it be placed in the north, the direction of elemental Earth, to represent the concrete realization of Mary's purpose? Or should it be located in the south, on elemental Fire, to express the force of her will fulfilled? It might even be located in the east, on elemental Air, since the work involves intellectual activity, and Air is the element of the intellect. Or in the west, on elemental Water, since that is the element of desire and the ritual involves an achievement she desires strongly. Mary decides to put the triangle in the south, the direction of Fire and the will, as the accompanying diagram shows.

Having chosen the cards that will serve as the active components in her ritual, Mary finds a quiet room where she will not be disturbed that has a table and chair where she can sit comfortably and lay out her cards. She divides the cards into piles so that she can reach them easily without hesitation, and sorts each pile into the order in which its cards will be laid out. One pile contains the four Aces of the altar. Another pile contains the twelve zodiacal trumps of the circle. Another holds the three elemental trumps of the triangle. Another has the three realizer cards that will go on the triangle. Another contains the three modifiers that will go on the circle. She also has the two significators, one for herself and the other to stand for the editor who will make the decision whether or not to award her the illustration contract.

If she needs help in remembering the astrological associations for the cards, and where they should be placed, Mary can write the associations down on a piece of paper and draw the layout, then put this sheet beside her for reference during the ritual. It is better to memorize all the Golden Dawn Tarot correspondences, but in the beginning you will probably not remember everything, and there is no shame in making notes as an aid to memory, merely for placing the cards in their correct locations in the ritual layout. This can be done during the planning of the ritual.

NORTH

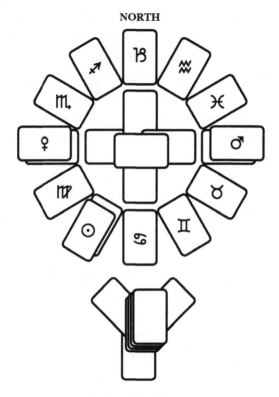

Business Ritual Layout

Mary sits quietly and stills her thoughts, making her mind alert and receptive. She takes several slow, deep breaths to cleanse her body and to help relax her muscles. She does not think directly about the stages of the ritual. These have more power if the mind of the magician does not dwell on them before they are carried out. She has seated herself in the west, facing east, to make visualizing herself on the astral level a bit easier, as the sideways orientation of her significator on the altar in the diagram indicates. The significator is always upright from the magician's position.

Taking up the pile of cards that contains the Aces of the altar, she lays them out in order: the Ace of Swords in the east, the Ace of Wands in the south, the Ace of Cups in the west, the Ace of Pentacles in the north. Interlacing the bases of the cards so that they are tipped, and stand up from the surface of the table slightly, she places her own significator, the Queen of Wands, upon the altar so that it is upright from her perspective.

Entering her significator on the astral level, so that in her imagination she seems to stand upon the rug of the significator upon the raised dais that supports the four rugs of the altar, she faces the east and spreads her arms so that her astral body forms a great cross, then performs the establishment of the altar in the astral place of working, centering herself on the altar.

"The heart of the four." (touch significator)

"The Sword before me, the Cup behind me, the Pentacle on my left hand, the Wand on my right hand." (touch each Ace in turn)

"The center of the universe." (touch significator)

She visualizes a great cross of light extending itself from her heart center to pierce the four emblems of the suits that float upon the air at the bases of the rugs of the four Aces.

Taking up the pile of cards that contains the twelve trumps of the zodiac, Mary lays them around the altar on the table, beginning with the Emperor on Aries in the east, and proceeding clockwise. If the proportions of the cards she is using permit it, she lays out the circle so that the corners of the cards touch, and they are closely gathered around the altar. Only if the cards are uncommonly long and narrow may the circle be slightly small for the altar, and have to be expanded. She does not worry if the circle is a bit irregular, or if there are gaps between the cards. What is imperfect in the material world can be made perfect in the astral world.

Having laid out the physical circle, she constructs the astral circle around herself as she stands in her astral form upon the altar of the four Aces.

"The One in All." (touch significator)

"The Emperor, the Hierophant, the Lovers, the Chariot, Strength, the Hermit, Justice, Death, Temperance, the Devil, the Star, the Moon." (touch each trump in turn)

"The circle is complete." (touch Emperor)

"The All in One." (touch significator)

Touching her significator with the tip of her right index finger, she simultaneously touches herself on the chest over her heart center on the astral level with her right hand. As she taps each trump and speaks its name, she points from her astral body at the glowing rectangle that floats in the air above its rug and projects into the rectangle the symbol of the zodiac sign of the trump. To complete the erection of the circle on the astral level, she again touches the significator on the altar with her right index finger, and simultaneously touches herself on the chest with her right hand in her astral body. A circle of golden light expands from her heart center to link all twelve signs of the zodiac surrounding the altar.

Taking up the three planetary modifiers, Mary lays them out clockwise upon their ruling signs, beginning with the Tower on the Emperor (Aries), followed by the Sun on Strength (Leo), then by the Empress on Justice (Libra). She taps each modifier in turn with her right index finger, establishing them on the astral level by projecting their planetary symbols into the rectangles of the signs they occupy. As she taps each modifier, she speaks its name.

"The Tower, the Sun, the Empress."

She visualizes the symbols of the planets floating above the symbols of the signs in their rectangles on the astral circle. In this way, the circle is energized by the modifiers for the purpose of the ritual.

Taking up the three elemental trumps of the triangle, she lays out the triangle in the south roughly a card length away from the circle, so that the Fool points toward the south. The cards are placed counterclockwise around the points of the triangle, first the Fool, then the Hanged Man, and finally Judgement, their bases interlaced so that they stand up slightly from the surface of the table. Upon the triangle she lays one by one the three realizer cards in reverse order so that they form a sequence from top to bottom

that expresses the order of the three stages of the ritual fulfillment. First is placed the Six of Cups, then the Four of Wands, and
then the Three of Pentacles.

On top of the pile of the three realizers on the triangle, Mary
puts the final card of the layout, the King of Cups, the significator that represents the editor whom she wishes to decide in her
favor when he awards the contract for the book illustrations.

To create the triangle on the astral level, she touches the three
elemental trumps in turn with her right index finger, beginning
with the Fool and moving counterclockwise. As she touches each,
she speaks its name.

"The Fool, the Hanged Man, Judgement."

Again, she touches the Fool to close the triangle, and speaks
the words:

"The triangle is prepared."

Gazing at the King of Cups on the triangle, in her imagination
she sees on the astral level a triangle of golden light floating upon
the air above the triangular dais that supports the three rugs of
the elemental trumps. Mary gathers her will, focusing her determination with the force of her desire on the purpose she wishes to
achieve. She takes a minute or so to allow the power of her will to
accumulate its energy, not forcing the process but letting it happen naturally while keeping her mind balanced and neutral. The
desire rises below the level of her conscious thought, of its own accord. It is like the spinning of a dynamo as it gathers momentum.

As an aid in this process of accumulating the force of her will,
she imagines the air of the astral circle swirling sunwise around
her as she stands on the altar, and glowing with a faint radiance.
It turns faster and faster, like a whirlwind that has its focus upon
her heart center, winding itself ever more tightly inward.

Sensing that the moment to trigger the ritual has arrived, Mary touches her significator on the altar with her right index finger, saying:

"The purpose is willed."

She concentrates her mind strongly on the person represented by the King of Cups on the altar to fill her imagination with his identity. Mentally she voices the name of the editor, and extends her mind to feel a link with that person. She is aware of the circle fully charged with the energy of her purpose.

Touching her right index finger to the significator on the triangle, she says:

"The purpose is fulfilled."

At the same time, she releases the accumulated energy of desire and intention from her heart center, where it is focused. She uses her right hand to draw it from the center of her chest and direct it in the form of a lance of light through the center of the triangle of golden fire that floats upright upon the air above the three elemental trumps. Bright white radiance fills the astral triangle, and the whirling air in the circle falls still.

Mary allows herself to briefly hold in her mind the three stages of her ritual purpose—the gaining of the contract, the completion of the contract, and the success the completion of the contract brings—as she contemplates the glowing triangle with her astral vision. She combines these three stages so that they are a single mingled desire, then abruptly lets the intention pass from her mind and turns her thoughts away from it.

She gathers up the cards in the reverse of the order in which they were laid out, first the King of Cups and the three realizers beneath it, then the three elemental trumps of the triangle, then the three planetary modifiers on the circle, followed by the cards of the circle itself, and finally her own significator followed by the

Aces of the altar. The gathered cards of the layout are shuffled into the rest of the Tarot deck, and the deck is put away for its next use.

Mary completely turns her mind away from the purpose of the ritual, releasing its energy. Whenever her thoughts return to it, she gently directs them to some other subject. She holds the unarticulated awareness that the purpose of the ritual has been wholly and perfectly fulfilled, but she does not think about it directly or brood about it. Much of the success of the ritual depends on how well she is able to release the ritual purpose from her mind after the ritual has been done. Her desire has been sent like an arrow to its target, and so is no longer a part of her. The ritual purpose will fulfill itself, in its own way and its own time.

TAROT CARD CHARMS

The general ritual procedure described in the preceding chapter can be used to create Tarot charms charged with occult potency for the realization of sustained purposes, such as providing protection or attracting love. The charm is composed of realizer cards expressing the objective of the charm. The cards are energized on the triangle, then kept together as a group rather than being shuffled back into the deck immediately following the ritual. The charm may be carried on the person or concealed in a place where it is needed.

This is not a permanent charm, but it is intended for a specific duration of use, at the end of which the cards are returned to the deck and lose their link with the charm. For example, if you wished to make a Tarot charm that caused you to be witty and attractive at a party you are planning to attend, you would create the charm with a Tarot ritual and would carry the charm in your pocket or hidden somewhere else in your clothing during the party. At the end of the evening, the cards of the charm would be shuffled back into the Tarot deck, bringing the power of the charm to an end. Or suppose you wished to protect your house while you are away on vacation. You could create a charm of protection for that purpose and conceal it somewhere near the center of the house. When you returned home, you would remove the charm from its place of hiding and return the cards to the deck.

The main reason for limiting the working span of these Tarot charms is that every time you make one, you separate several number cards from the deck and render the deck unsuitable for other uses until the cards are put back into it. Another reason is the inherent fragility of cards. They are not made for prolonged wearing on the body, and are easily damaged by handling, perspiration, and oil from the skin. By their very nature, cards are multipurpose. They do not have a single function in Tarot magic, but are made to serve many functions. If a permanent charm is needed, it is better to construct it out of some durable material using more conventional methods of ceremonial magic.

These Tarot charms have the advantage over conventional charms in that they cost nothing in materials since you already have a deck of Tarot cards, they do not require you to obtain or gather obscure substances for the composition of the charm, and they can be assembled and charged in a brief time with no preparation. If you wish, you can make or buy a folder such as a small wallet specifically for holding and carrying Tarot charms. Something such as a rigid cigarette case would give the cards of the charm added protection from accidental damage. However, a plain paper envelope will serve the same purpose just as well, provided you take care not to bend or otherwise damage the cards.

In an ordinary ritual, such as the ritual to obtain a business contract described as an example in the previous chapter, you use your will as a psychic lance to open the gateway in the triangle to the higher level of universal spirit where magic finds its realization. The realizer cards on the triangle act as a template to shape your will into a form that accurately expresses your ritual purpose. The realization of the purpose immediately reflects from this higher level of spirit, which exists above the astral level, down to the material world where it plays itself out in your life. The cards on the triangle are used to shape and guide the energy of your magical desire, but they are not themselves the focus of that desire.

When making a charm, the cards on the triangle become the focus. The purpose of a charm-making ritual is to charge a set of cards with a specific occult potential, in much the same way a battery is charged with electrical potential, so that if and when the charm is needed, its accumulated power will flow forth to accomplish its function. The procedure is the same; only the intention is different. The cards of the charm, placed as realizers on the triangle, embody the purpose, which is the creation of a particular kind of charm. They are held in the mind during the final phase of the ritual when energy is sent lancing into the triangle to open the gateway of the Fool. The reflux of occult energy from the level of universal spirit expresses itself by energizing the cards of the charm, rather than by accomplishing some other specific task.

It is the intention in the mind of the magician, symbolized in material form in the sequence of realizer cards that make up the charm on the triangle, that determines how the lance of will released at the end of the ritual expresses itself. The power sent forth from the ritual place on the astral level always rebounds down to the material level to fulfill itself, but how it fulfills itself is controlled by the ritual purpose. If it is to gain a business contract, it will express itself in the material world by causing events that bring about the offering of the contract to the magician; but if it is to create a Tarot charm, it will express itself by charging the cards sitting on the physical triangle.

The number of cards used to compose a charm should be limited for the sake of simplicity and purity of result. Too many cards will conflict with each other, and weaken the working of the charm. One is a good number for a charm, as is three. More than three cards is not a good idea, except for the inclusion of a significator, which does not bear on the number of realizers that make up the charm. A significator included in the charm can be useful in focusing and limiting the action of the charm on an individual, when the charm is deliberately created for the benefit of a single person, or to affect only a single person. Some charms are general, others specific. A general charm does not require a significator, but a charm made for one person can be more narrowly focused if a significator representing that person is included in the charm.

The same principles that apply to the use of realizer cards in general also apply to charms. The significator, if one is used, should be on top of the pile that is placed on the triangle. The number cards of the charm, when more than a single realizer is used, are ordered from top to bottom in the sequence of desired events that express the successful working of the charm. The cards are placed on the triangle one by one, in reverse order to their working. That is to say, the realizer card that is the last stage in the working of the charm is placed first on the triangle, because it goes on the bottom, and the cards are stacked from bottom to top. When a significator is used, it is always the final card to be placed on the triangle.

After the charm is charged, it is taken off the triangle as a group of cards. This is contrary to the usual way the cards are taken up after a ritual. The usual practice is to take up the cards one by one in the reverse order to which they were laid out. Since the cards of the charm form a single entity after being empowered by the ritual, they must be kept together in the same order. Never separate the cards of the charm or mix up their sequence after the charm is ritually charged, or you will end its effectiveness. Take them up from the triangle as a group and immediately place them in the envelope that will hold them, or into whatever other container you have prepared for them.

Do not spend time looking at the charm, or thinking about it after the ritual. Try to create the sense that you know, below the level of thought or doubt, that the charm has been rightly made and is doing its job. Be as relaxed and confident about this as you are that the sun will rise in the morning. It is so certain a thing, you do not need to wonder if it is true. Its truth is self-evident. When something is so true that no one would ever think of questioning it, there is no reason to doubt its reality. This is the mind state you must achieve following the ritual to charge a Tarot charm if you wish the charm to function unhindered—for your doubt concerning its effectiveness will act as an impediment to its action. The more you doubt, the weaker you will make the charm by frustrating its natural working.

This may seem to be no more than a trick of the mind, but that is what all magic is—a way of shaping the condition of the unconscious mind so that desired effects are realized in the world. All magic is done in the mind. The physical instruments of ritual are merely tools for shaping and directing the unconscious mind. The conscious mind cannot bring about an effect in magic; it can merely aid in shaping the unconscious mind in a way that will produce the effect. It is another tool, as are the will and the emotions. Belief is the most potent of all tools. In religion it is called faith, in magic it is called belief. It is the mental condition of knowing a thing is true with such certainty that the impulse to doubt never arises.

EXAMPLE OF A GOOD LUCK CHARM

To demonstrate by example how a Tarot charm is made, suppose that you are going antique hunting with your friends and wish to find a good bargain. You decide to create a charm for good luck the night before that you can carry with you as you travel from antique shop to antique shop. Since there is no individual connected with the charm other than yourself, a second significator is not needed. You decide to use three realizer cards in your charm to express the nature of the good luck you are seeking.

After some thought, you choose for your charm three number cards that stand for three stages in your purpose.

The first stage is to locate something desirable, or something for which you have long been searching. This will entail traveling from shop to shop, and will call upon the keenness of your perceptions. One choice for this first stage in obtaining the good fortune you seek is the Six of Swords, titled the Lord of Earned Success. The card signifies earned success after effort, and also safe travel, particularly over water. Even if the afternoon of antique hunting will not entail much crossing of water, the association of successful travel in general is appropriate. Its decanate is the second in Aquarius, ruled by Mercury, the planet that presides over money matters, and also has to do with the quickness of the mind. This card is also associated with the astrological Sun in Tiphareth on the Tree of Life, a fortunate combination of factors.

The second stage in the action of the charm, once an object has been located, is its acquisition. For this an appropriate card is the Eight of Pentacles, titled the Lord of Prudence. It signifies wise handling of money, and also the finding of hidden wealth or objects. In general, the suit of Pentacles is suitable for material acquisitions. This card presides over the first decanate of Virgo, ruled by the astrological planet the Sun. It is also linked with Mercury in Hod. The appearance of Mercury again in this second card is auspicious for the purpose of the charm. Virgo signified prudent management of resources.

The third stage of the charm, after the acquisition of the desired object, is the enjoyment of its possession untroubled by any misgivings or unhappy revelations. For this phase, the Nine of Cups is an excellent choice. It is titled the Lord of Material Happiness, and signifies perfect satisfaction and the fulfillment of a wish. This card presides over the second decanate of Pisces, ruled by Jupiter, and also the astrological Moon in the sphere of Yesod. To some extent, this happiness will be more perceived than actual, which is to say it will be based on an emotional reaction to the object acquired rather than on its intrinsic monetary value, but it will be no less satisfying because it is subjective rather than objective.

The planetary modifiers on the zodiacal circle are located by keying them to the planets that rule the decanates of the realizer cards, and placing them on the signs of the zodiac ruled by those planets.

The Six of Swords, linked with Mercury in the second decanate of Aquarius, receives as its modifier the planetary trump the Magician, which corresponds with Mercury. This is placed in either of the zodiac signs ruled by Mercury, which are Gemini and Virgo.

The Eight of Pentacles, linked with the Sun in the first decanate of Virgo, receives as its modifier the planetary trump the Sun, which corresponds with the astrological Sun. This is placed in the single sign ruled by the Sun, which is Leo.

The Nine of Cups, linked with Jupiter in the second decanate of Pisces, receives as its modifier the planetary trump the Wheel, which corresponds with Jupiter. This is placed in either of the zodiac signs ruled by Jupiter, which are Sagittarius and Pisces.

In determining where to place the modifiers, we start with the trump the Sun because it rules only one sign, Leo, and no choice is necessary. When we locate the Magician and the Wheel, which sign should be selected is determined largely by the aspects that will be created. We wish harmonious or fortunate aspects between the three modifiers, if this is possible.

The Magician placed on the Hermit (Virgo) creates a semi-sextile aspect with the trump of the Sun on Strength (Leo), and this is a weak aspect. If we place the Magician on the other sign ruled by Mercury, the Lovers (Gemini), a sextile aspect is formed, a much stronger and more favorable aspect. The final modifier, the Wheel, can go on either Temperance (Sagittarius) or the trump the Moon (Pisces). Temperance would put it in trine with the trump the Sun, but in opposition with the Magician. However, if we place it on the other choice, the trump the Moon, we form no aspect with the trump the Sun on Leo, and the undesirable square aspect with the Magician on Gemini.

A workable choice for the modifiers is the trump the Sun on the sign Leo (Strength), the trump the Magician on the sign Gemini (Lovers), and the trump the Wheel on the sign Sagittarius (Temperance). Always bear in mind that you can place the modifiers anywhere on the circle of the zodiac, and can select as many or as few modifiers as you wish. The mechanical system of selecting the modifiers according to the ruling planets in the decanates of the realizers is merely a simple way of choosing them that automatically avoids serious conflicts.

Beginners should not be intimidated by the modifiers. They are the most complex part of Tarot magic, but understanding their use is not difficult once you become familiar with the planets that rule the signs of the zodiac, and with the choice of aspects when placing them. It is possible to work successful rituals, and to make potent and effective charms, without the planetary modifiers. They help channel the energies of the rituals but are not essential to their fulfillment. If you are baffled by the use of the modifiers, leave them out of your rituals until you come to understand their use.

You will notice that in constructing the charm, no attempt is made to specify what object will be acquired, how much money it will cost, or where it will be located. The function of the charm is general—to give good luck in antique hunting. Were an attempt made to narrow down its working, it would become less effective. Magic needs room to find its own way to achieve its ends. It cannot be bullied or driven along a narrow path. It is a principle of magic that the more conditions or constraints are placed upon its working, the less likely it is to succeed. In using this charm, you will get the best results if you do not think about carrying it with you, and do not think about what antique you might find in your travels. Any particular expectation would act to limit the charm, and thus weaken it.

The ritual is laid out in the same way as the ritual of the previous chapter, which gives the general full ritual layout of Tarot magic. The only difference is that the triangle is placed in the north, the quarter of elemental Earth and a good choice for a charm designed to result in a material acquisition. The words spoken are the same. It is possible to construct unique Tarot rituals for every purpose, but in this book I have deliberately given a general ritual pattern that can be used for any purpose. The specific intention that directs the will for the accomplishment of the ritual desire is held in the mind, and shaped by the realizer cards and the modifier cards, so a unique wording of the ritual text is not required.

After you have constructed the ritual layout with the cards, and have activated it on the astral level using the ritual words and the power of visualization, hold the purpose of the ritual, which is the creation of the charm, in your mind and allow your desire for its attainment to build naturally, below the surface of your conscious awareness. It is something you want, so the desire will build by itself if you allow it to accumulate without distraction—there is no need

NORTH

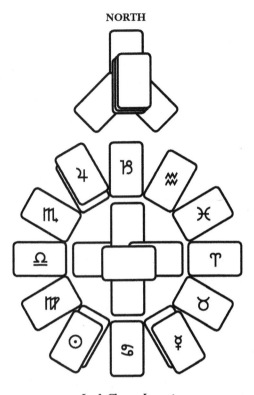

Luck Charm Layout

to try to force-feed the desire. Strive for clarity of focus in your mind. Consider the three cards on the triangle, and their function, all the while sharpening the lance of your will.

When you feel that enough energy has been accumulated in the astral circle, hurl that lance of will with your right hand from your heart center through the upright astral triangle of light that floats in the air above the three rugs of the elemental trumps on the triangular dais. Mentally watch the upright triangle fill with bright radiance, and watch it slowly fade. Take up the three realizer cards that are the charm for good luck and place them in your container, which can be as simple as a new envelope of white paper. Then pick up the cards of the layout one by one in the reverse order to which they were laid out and shuffle them back into the Tarot deck. The ritual is ended, but the charm continues to exist, and continues to hold its charge of occult energy. It will fulfill its purpose when given the opportunity to do so.

The charm should not be kept intact for longer than, at most, a few weeks. It is best to make Tarot charms for a single day of use. Their action is most effective when the charm is brought into contact or at least close proximity with what it is designed to act on. A charm of protection should be carried by the person it is created to protect. A charm of good fortune should be placed where the good fortune is needed. A love charm directed at a particular individual should be brought near or into contact with that individual, without that person being made aware of the existence of the charm.

Magic works best in secret. Never tell anyone that you have worked a ritual or made a charm. Do not boast that you are going to accomplish some purpose using magic. In fact, do not talk about your Tarot magic at all. If you make a charm to act on someone, it is much better if that person never knows anything about it. Their awareness of the charm, even if they have the best intentions, is likely to hinder the working of the charm.

26

EVOKING AN ELEMENTAL

An elemental spirit is called forth to perceptible presence, or evoked, within the triangle using the same general ritual that serves to establish a sustained communication with a living person, or with the soul of a person who has died. In all three instances, the goal is to forge a link with another intelligent being. Calling forth the elemental into the triangle creates a separation between the magician and the spirit, who occupy the astral place on opposite sides of the magic circle. The channel of communication is established through the vortex at the center of the altar, and the vortex at the center of the triangle, which are connected on the higher level of spirit above the astral level. It is not possible for the elemental to travel through these point doorways and gain entrance into the circle, unless you deliberately open the way for the spirit and explicitly invite the spirit into the circle.

Each of the number cards from Two to Ten in the four suits of the Lesser Arcana has its own elemental spirit. The nature of the spirit is defined by the function of the card. For example, the Three of Cups is associated with pleasant society, hospitality, feasting, celebration, and finery. These functions determine the personality of the spirit of the Three of Cups, who is cheerful, friendly, and fond of display and adornment. The general or public name of the elemental associated with a number card is the same as the title of the card. The undine of the Three of Cups is called the Lord of Abundance when the spirit appears in masculine form, but the Lady of Abundance when the spirit appears in feminine form.

An elemental of a number card, when it takes on human form in the triangle, can appear either male or female. Both sexes exist in potential in these spirits, who are of a dual nature. It is simplest to think of each card as having two ruling spirits, a lord and a lady. The magician keys the ritual to either the lord or lady of the number card on the triangle by conceiving the sex of the spirit and voicing the spirit's title during the evocation. You will find when you think about each of these elemental spirits, that the spirit naturally tends to assume a gender best expressing the nature of the spirit as you conceive it. You should accept that gender rather than attempting to force the elemental to take on the opposite sex.

Some elements are naturally feminine, and others naturally masculine. The feminine elements are Water and Earth. Spirits of these elements will have feminine characteristics even when they are evoked in male form. The masculine elements are Fire and Air. Spirits of these elements will tend to exhibit masculine qualities even when outwardly female. The sexual bias is most strongly present in Fire, which is predominantly masculine in nature, and Water, which is predominantly feminine. Air and Earth are of a mixed nature, so the gender difference in the spirits of these elements is less distinct.

The circle must be strongly infused with the element of the spirit you seek to evoke, if the ritual is to be successful. This is done in several ways.

The color of the element of the spirit evoked is employed during the ritual to create harmony with the spirit. During most rituals, the cross of light extended from the chest when centering yourself and energizing the altar is imagined as pale gold in color, but during evocation rituals it should be conceived as the color of the element of the spirit. The same is true for the expanded circle of light, and for the radiant triangle of light that floats on the air above the three elemental trumps of the triangle.

Red is the color of Wands and Fire. Blue is the color of Cups and Water. Yellow is the color of Swords and Air. Green is the color of Pentacles and Earth. The yellow of Air should be thought of as deep and rich, much darker than the pale gold of spiritual radiance. The primary Golden Dawn color for Earth is black, but black is not very workable as a color for beams of light during rituals, so I prefer to use a deep green for Earth. This is acceptable because the Golden Dawn acknowledged four colors for elemental Earth—citrine, russet, olive, and sable.

The circle is further infused with the element of the spirit by moving your own significator from the center of the altar toward the arm of the altar cross that corresponds with the element. It should continue to cover the center of the altar, but be shifted toward the arm of the cross of the element, so that its action is weighted in favor of that single element. For example, if you wish to evoke a salamander, or Fire elemental, lay your significator so that it projects more over the Ace of Wands than over any of the other Aces. Your significator is still oriented upright from your own perspective, but its center has shifted toward one of the arms of the altar.

The circle is made to resonate even more strongly with the element of the spirit by laying on top of its trine of zodiac signs the three planetary modifiers that rule those signs.

Fire Trine
Aries (Emperor) ruled by planet Mars (Tower)
Leo (Strength) ruled by planet the Sun (Sun)
Sagittarius (Temperance) ruled by planet Jupiter (Wheel)

Water Trine
Cancer (Chariot) ruled by planet the Moon (High Priestess)
Scorpio (Death) ruled by planet Mars (Tower)
Pisces (the Moon) ruled by planet Jupiter (Wheel)

Air Trine

Libra (Justice) ruled by planet Venus (Empress)
Aquarius (Star) ruled by planet Saturn (World)
Gemini (Lovers) ruled by planet Mercury (Magician)

Earth Trine

Capricorn (Devil) ruled by planet Saturn (World)
Taurus (Hierophant) ruled by planet Venus (Empress)
Virgo (Hermit) ruled by planet Mercury (Magician)

The three planetary modifiers placed over the trine of signs associated with a single element naturally form trine aspects, so that their combined influence is in perfect harmony. The use of the planetary modifiers of a single element on the circle, coupled with the placement of your own significator over the Ace of that element on the altar, saturates the circle with the element and makes the ritual layout attractive to spirits of that element.

The advantage of summoning the elemental spirit of a number card, rather than simply working a ritual to accomplish the desired purpose, is that an elemental is a conscious being able to adapt to changing circumstances and solve problems that relate to its function. A ritual constructed incorrectly may fail to achieve its purpose, but when an elemental is summoned, the magician can simply tell it what must be accomplished and the elemental will use its own ingenuity and initiative to achieve the objective. The more often a spirit is summoned, the easier it is to call forth, and the more effective its actions.

The elemental of a number card is a simple being. Its purpose is encompassed by the nature of the card to which it is attached. It is a thinking, active embodiment of the card, with an innate urge to fulfill the function of the card. That is its reason to exist. Elementals of the number cards are eager to act for the magician since in this way they fulfill themselves. Care must be taken not to ask an elemental to do a thing it is unsuited to accomplish, since this will only result in frustration and failure. It is necessary to understand your purpose and to know which realizer card is best suited to fulfill that task before summoning the elemental of the card.

The form of the evoked elemental, and how clearly you are able to perceive the spirit on the astral level, depends on how well you understand the nature of the number card from which it is summoned, and how open your mind is to psychic impressions. It is best not to start with a detailed concept of the appearance of the spirit. The first time you summon a particular elemental you will know in advance its gender and title, and will have some preconception of its overall appearance, and perhaps a few details such as hair and eye color, but you should allow the rest of its form and personality to take shape as you continue to work with the spirit.

Similarly, whether the elemental answers your instructions in words that you are able to hear on the astral level depends on your own psychic development. Many magicians never hear the words of elemental spirits, or see their forms clearly, even after working with elementals for years. It is not necessary to see and hear an elemental before you can give the spirit instructions. The evoked spirit will have no trouble at all seeing you and hearing every word you utter, either aloud or in your thoughts. Do not assume that your evocation has failed merely because the triangle seems empty. Often the spirit is present and waiting for you to tell it what to do, although it may remain invisible to your sight.

A useful extended ritual working for serious Tarot magicians is to evoke all thirty-six elementals of the number cards on successive nights, one spirit on each night, and ask that spirit to tell you its true secret name. The title of the card is the public name of the elemental attached to it, but it also has a private name that you may use to summon it. This secret name can only be learned from the spirit itself, by asking the spirit to reveal it to you. The name will be specific to you—another magician asking for the secret name would get another response. It is akin to a mantra passed from master to disciple, unique to each circumstance. Its revelation is both an expression of trust by the spirit, and a kind of compact between the spirit and the magician to whom the name is given.

Have a pen and paper nearby during the ritual of evocation. Ask the spirit for its true name, and then keep your mind receptive. The name will come as if from the depths of your unconscious. Unless you are uncommonly mediumistic, you will not hear it spoken with your ears. You must be alert to distinguish between a received name and the vague currents of your own subjective thought processes. A name placed in your mind by the spirit you have summoned will resonate more strongly than your own thoughts, and will have a sense of rightness. It will seem the most appropriate possible name for that spirit.

EXAMPLE OF ELEMENTAL EVOCATION

The best way to explain the general ritual procedure of elemental evocation is to run through a hypothetical example. Let us assume that you have had a falling out with a close friend and wish to restore the friendship to its former state. The friend refuses to respond to your phone calls or e-mail messages. You could conduct a ritual of communion and try to persuade your friend directly by projecting your thoughts into your friend's mind through a psychic link, but you decide to use an elemental spirit to repair the relationship. You choose as your spiritual agent the elemental of the Two of Swords.

Your own intuitive perception of this spirit is that she is female, so you modify her title, calling her the Lady of Peace Restored. You conceive her initially much as she is depicted on this card in the Rider-Waite Tarot, as a slender woman with short dark hair who wears a long white robe that hangs down to her feet. She is not blindfolded, as she appears on the Waite card, nor does she carry swords. These symbolic details on Waite's version of the card are only intended to indicate A. E. Waite's concept of the card, and are not inevitable features of the elemental spirit of the card. This description is intended only as an example—another magician might well see the spirit differently.

The altar is erected in the usual way on the table, with the Ace of Swords pointing toward the east. You sit on the west side, facing east. Your significator is placed, not in the center of the altar as is usual for most rituals, but partially over the Ace of Swords, because this evocation concerns a sylph, and Air elementals are of the suit of Swords.

Visualize yourself in the astral space, standing on the raised dais of the altar in the center, so that your feet are near the edge of the rug of your significator, which is misaligned to the east. You face east, arms spread wide.

Touch the tip of your right index finger to your significator and say the words:

"The heart of the four."

Touch in succession the Ace of Swords, Ace of Cups, Ace of Pentacles, and Ace of Wands, so that your finger describes a cross above the altar. As you touch the cards, say:

**"The Sword before me, the Cup behind me, the Pentacle
on my left hand, the Wand on my right hand."**

As you touch each Ace, visualize in the astral space the symbol of its suit materializing in the air above the end of its card-rug. Each symbol flickers and shines with a pale golden radiance.

Again, touch your significator with your fingertip and say the words:

"The center of the universe."

Visualize a cross composed of deep yellow beams extending itself outward in the four directions from your heart center. It is colored deep yellow tinged slightly with green, the citrine of elemental Air, because your significator has been shifted toward the eastern arm of the altar cross, creating an elemental imbalance. Each beam pierces the symbol of its suit. Mentally lower your arms and contemplate this cross for several moments, then allow it to fade from your imagination.

Lay out the circle of the zodiac in the usual way. With the tip of your right index finger, touch your significator on the altar. Visualize yourself on the astral level, standing on the center of the altar facing east, and imagine that you touch your chest with your right hand as you say these words:

"The All in One."

Touch each card of the circle in turn with your right index finger, beginning with the Emperor and proceeding clockwise. As you touch each trump, speak its name:

"The Emperor, the Hierophant, the Lovers, the Chariot, Strength, the Hermit, Justice, Death, Temperance, the Devil, the Star, the Moon."

Visualize yourself on the astral level, pointing in turn with your right hand at the glowing golden rectangles of light that float above each zodiacal trump as you slowly turn clockwise on your own axis. When you utter each name, mentally project the symbol of its sign into the rectangle in pale golden light. See each symbol clearly before moving on to the next trump.

Touch the trump the Emperor once again to close the circle, and speak the words:

"The circle is complete."

Touch the significator again, and at the same time imagine that you touch your chest over your heart with your right hand as you stand in your astral body on the altar. Speak the words:

"The One in All."

NORTH

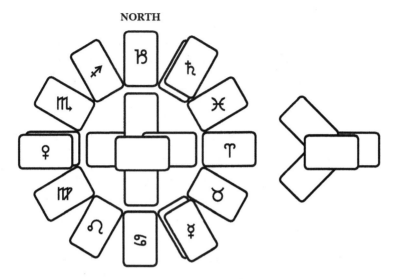

Elemental Evocation Layout

Imagine a ring of deep yellow expanding from your heart center through the air to link all twelve signs of the zodiac in their rectangles above the rugs of the trumps. It is the citrine of elemental Air.

Lay the three planetary modifiers that rule the signs of the trine of elemental Air on the circle clockwise, beginning with the Cardinal Air sign, Libra, then the Fixed Air sign, Aquarius, and finally the Mutable Air sign, Gemini. Libra is ruled by Venus, so the zodiacal trump Justice (Libra) is covered with the modifier trump the Empress (Venus). Aquarius is ruled by Saturn, so the zodiacal trump the Star (Aquarius) is covered with the modifier trump the World (Saturn). Gemini is ruled by Mercury, so the zodiacal trump the Lovers (Gemini) is covered by the modifier trump the Magician (Mercury).

When the three planetary modifiers have been laid on the zodiacal circle, touch each with your right index finger in the order in which they were laid out, moving clockwise around the circle. As each modifier is tapped with your fingertip, speak its name:

"The Empress, the World, the Magician."

As you speak the name of each modifier, imagine yourself standing on the astral altar, and point at the rectangle of light above the zodiacal trump that modifier occupies. Mentally project in deep yellow the symbol of the planet of the modifier into the rectangle so that the symbol of the planet floats above the symbol of the sign.

Build the triangle of realization on the eastern side of the circle, the direction of elemental Air and the suit of Swords. Lay upon it the Two of Swords so that the number card is centered on the triangle, with its base pointing toward the center of the circle.

Visualize yourself standing on the dais of the astral altar, facing the triangle in the east. Touch with your right fingertip the three trumps of the triangle in turn counterclockwise around the triangle, saying their names:

"The Fool, the Hanged Man, Judgement."

Again, touch the Fool to close the triangle. Say the words:

"The triangle is prepared."

Imagine an upright triangle of deep yellow light form itself on the air about a foot above the dais that supports the interwoven rugs of the elemental trumps. It is the same yellow Air color as the cross and the circle.

Concentrate your mind strongly on the elemental spirit of the Two of Swords. As you hold in your awareness the nature of the elemental, which you conceive as a slender woman with short dark hair who wears a long white gown, mentally voice the title of the spirit, the Lady of Peace Restored. Feel that spirit drawing closer to the circle, aware of your presence.

Touch your own significator on the altar with your right index finger, saying:

"The purpose is willed."

Charge the circle with the energy of your intention. On the astral level, imagine that the strengthening power of your will creates a swirling sunwise whirlwind of light that is colored a transparent citrine and has its focus on your heart center.

Touch with your right index finger the Two of Swords on the triangle, saying:

"The purpose is fulfilled."

At once release your gathered will toward the elemental spirit. Cast it away from you using your right hand and arm as though flinging a yellow lance of lightning into the center of the triangle of light. Visualize the upright astral triangle fill with a deep citrine.

Again touch your own significator in the center of the zodiacal circle with your index finger, saying:

"The way is open."

Visualize on the astral level a returning bolt of yellow light emerging from the upright triangle to flash into your heart center. It is immediately reflected and darts back to the triangle. This pulse of light flies back and forth, faster and faster, for several seconds until it forms a solid beam of yellow light between your chest and the upright triangle. Not only imagine seeing this reciprocal pulse, but feel it in your astral body.

The blinding yellow radiance filling the upright triangle gradually fades, allowing you to see the elemental spirit, the Lady of Peace Restored, who stands upon the center of the triangular dais, framed in the upright triangle as though in an open doorway of light. How clearly you see her will depend on your level of psychic talent, coupled with your skill in visualizing astral forms. Even if you see nothing, keep your mind receptive to any impressions that may arise. If you get the sense of a particular shape or color framed in the triangle, allow your mind to create it on the astral level. It is probably the elemental spirit attempting to reveal herself to your awareness.

You converse with the sylph on the triangle by speaking silently in your own mind, forming your words with great clarity so that they almost seem audible to your ears. Tell the spirit what you wish the spirit to do. In the case of the example, the Lady of Peace Restored is instructed to go to the friend with whom you have had an argument, and persuade the friend that you wish the friendship resumed, and bear no ill feeling toward the other person.

When you get the inner sense that the elemental has understood your instructions, withdraw your mind, breaking the beam of light that connects you with the elemental. Take up the cards of the layout in reverse order to the way they were set down, and shuffle them back into the pack. Turn your mind away from the ritual, but have in the back of your thoughts the unexpressed conviction that the purpose of the ritual has been completely and perfectly realized. It is not something you need to think about because it is so certain.

The elemental will go to your former friend and use her powers of persuasion below the level of the person's conscious awareness, so that the person reconsiders the disagreement with you and decides to attempt a reconciliation. Your friend will probably be unaware of the spirit's presence. The elemental will not cease working until this fulfillment is achieved, because its achievement is the reason for the elemental's existence. The spirit will use its ingenuity to accomplish its purpose, taking advantage of any accidental circumstance that may arise. Eventually, the ritual purpose will be fulfilled, though not always in the way that was presupposed by the magician.

appendix

MODIFIED TAROT
CORRESPONDENCES

Having studied the Tarot for the past thirty years or so and having used it extensively for divination and practical magic, it is not surprising that I have formed my own opinion as to the most meaningful and potent sequence for the trumps, and what their esoteric associations should be. My personal arrangement is based on the Golden Dawn Tarot correspondences for the trumps, but departs from it in several significant ways. Although I have the highest respect for Samuel L. MacGregor Mathers as a magician and spirit medium, I do not look upon him as infallible.

The main original contribution by Mathers to the correspondences for the trumps was his ordering of the trumps linked to the seven Double letters of the Hebrew alphabet. The sequence of the planets on these seven letters was not made clear in the Kabbalistic text *Sepher Yetzirah*, opening it to later debate, and there has been considerable disagreement. The Golden Dawn sequence is that of the Secret Chiefs, psychically communicated to Mathers. I must disagree with the Secret Chiefs. My own sense is that since the zodiac signs are applied to the Hebrew Single letters in their natural order, the same should be true of the astrological planets on the Double letters. The order of the planets is based on their apparent speeds of progress across the night sky, when measured against the fixed backdrop of the stars from night to night. From quickest to slowest, the natural order is: Moon, Mercury, Venus, Sun, Mars, Jupiter, Saturn.

If this direct application of the planets to the trumps linked with the Double letters makes such sense, why did Mathers and the Secret Chiefs fail to adopt it? The answer is obvious when a comparison is made between the symbolism of the trumps and the planets. They do not fit together harmoniously. For example, to place the first astrological planet, the Moon, on the first Double letter would result in the planet the Moon being linked with the Magician. The Moon is a feminine planet, whereas the Magician is a strongly masculine trump. Similarly, the second planet in their natural order, Mercury, would fall on the trump the High Priestess. This also seems incorrect. Mercury is a masculine planet, and is associated with magic, but the High Priestess is a feminine trump and is associated with mystery.

Even so, I persist in my sense that the assignment of the planets to the Double letters should be in their natural order, just as is true of the zodiac signs. The three active elements cannot really be said to have an order, both because only three out of the four elements are represented, and because the elements change places constantly and may be ordered in several different ways, each equally valid. Their assignment, which is explicitly given in *Sepher Yetzirah*, need not be questioned.

The only answer to the problem of the planets is to modify the sequence of the trumps. There is ample precedent for this course. Court de Gébelin and Eliphas Lévi did it by locating the Fool at the beginning of the trumps. Mathers inverted the placements of Justice and Strength. Crowley inverted the Emperor with the Star. It cannot be presumed that all changes in the order of the trumps are necessary, or even prudent, but the evolution of the Tarot as an instrument of modern Western magic has been driven by these modifications in the ordering and esoteric associations for the trumps.

When the natural order of the planets is accepted as a desirable feature of the Tarot correspondences, and they are placed in order on the seven Double letters of the Hebrew alphabet, it remains to correctly assign the trumps that are linked to the Double letters by trading their locations in the sequence of trumps. It is at once obvious that the trump the Magician belongs with Mercury and the trump the High Priestess belongs with the Moon. Consequently, the Magician must be made the second of the planetary trumps and numbered II, and the High Priestess shifted into first place and numbered I. As I mentioned earlier, the trumps have no intrinsic numbers of their own, merely numbers that indicate their locations in the series of the Greater Arcana.

This is the most radical change I have made to the correspondences, and is apt to be the most controversial. The question may be asked by misogynists, "How can a woman come first, before a man?" Yet it will be noted that the Empress precedes the Emperor, and that a symmetry is created in the two pairs of trumps—High Priestess followed by Magician, and Empress followed by Emperor. The High Priestess does not actually assume the head of the trumps by this change of position, even though she is numbered I. That post is filled by the Fool, numbered 0, so a man still heads the trumps in an overt sense, even though esoterically the Fool is held to be sexually androgynous. We get the androgynous Fool, followed by the female High Priestess, then her natural mate the male Magician, then the female Empress, followed by her natural mate the male Emperor, followed by the androgynous Hierophant.

Venus is in her correct position on the Empress, who need not be moved. However, the trump of the next Double letter, the Wheel of Fortune, receives the planet Jupiter in the Golden Dawn correspondences. If the natural order of the planets is to be preserved, we must assign the astrological Sun to the trump the Wheel. And what could be a more perfect fit? The Sun is the great wheel of the heavens. It has been depicted in this way in the mythology of countless cultures. It is a good deal more appropriate, symbolically, than Jupiter.

Mars is in his correct position on the Tower, which does not need to be moved. When we come to the trump the Sun, which receives the astrological planet the Sun in the Golden Dawn correspondences, we must use another planet since the Sun has been linked to the Wheel of Fortune. The obvious choice is Jupiter, termed in astrology the Greater Fortune and renowned for its beneficence, and Jupiter falls here naturally in the order of planets.

Some critics may object that the most natural planet for the trump the Sun is surely the planet the Sun. Yet, if this is so, why is it that the planet the Moon is never assigned to the trump the Moon? It seems to me that either both Sun and Moon should be linked to the trumps that bear their names, or neither should be so linked. Since the astrological Moon has never been placed on the trump the Moon, I have no reluctance to associate the trump the Sun with the planet Jupiter.

The final planet in the natural order of the planets is Saturn. It is in its correct location at the end of the Double letters, and is appropriately linked with the trump the World.

These two changes to the Golden Dawn correspondences—inverting the locations of the trumps the Magician and the High Priestess along with their attached planets, and inverting the locations of the planets the Sun and Jupiter—create a relationship between the planets and the trumps of the Double letters that feels correct to me. If I were to stop there it would surely be radical enough, but there are assignments to the trumps of the Single letters in the Golden Dawn system that do not appear correct and must be modified, before I can accept that the best possible arrangement of the trumps has been achieved. I cannot shift the zodiac signs because they are in their natural order. It becomes necessary to invert pairs of trumps.

One trump that has long troubled me is Temperance. It has always felt out of place. We have the sequence of the dark and brooding trumps Justice, the Hanged Man, Death, the Devil, and the Tower, and in the midst of them we find the pleasant trump Temperance. To me it has always felt completely wrong. Add to this the zodiac sign associated with Temperance in the Golden Dawn correspondences, Sagittarius the Archer. I know that Mathers and others who commented on the Golden Dawn Tarot went to great lengths to justify the link between Temperance and Sagittarius in their writings. Much of what they wrote is plausible and persuasive. Even so, I have never been convinced.

There is another zodiacal trump that I find equally troubling, and it is the Chariot. It has always struck me as out of its natural place, coming as it does immediately after the Lovers and just before Strength. Why should so dark and bloody a trump fall in the midst of trumps that are peaceful and positive? My strong feeling is that it should not. Associated with the Chariot is Cancer the Crab. Again, an attempt has been made to justify this association, but I find no reason to accept it. Really, there is very little that is masculine and warlike about the sign of Cancer, in spite of countless references to the savage claws of the crustacean. I have never myself felt particularly threatened by crabs, which on the whole are harmless creatures.

My solution, as you may have suspected, is to invert the locations of the trumps the Chariot and Temperance. This inversion causes Temperance to fall immediately after the Lovers, and to receive the sign of Cancer. The Chariot falls in the midst of the dark trumps, immediately after Death, and it receives the zodiac sign of Sagittarius. To my mind, the warlike Archer is a much more appropriate zodiac sign for a trump of war than the Crab, particularly since chariots were used as mobile platforms for archers during war. On the other hand, feminine and nurturing Cancer seems well suited to Temperance. There is a natural yin-yang balance in the glyph of Cancer itself, which resembles the symbolism on the traditional version of the trump Temperance of two vessels linked by a stream of liquid.

Here is what I regard as the correct arrangement of the Tarot trumps, with their elemental and astrological correspondences. The sequence of Hebrew letters remains unaltered:

Aleph (Mother)	0 Fool (Air)
Beth (Double)	I High Priestess (Moon)
Gimel (Double)	II Magician (Mercury)
Daleth (Double)	III Empress (Venus)
Heh (Single)	IV Emperor (Aries)
Vau (Single)	V Hierophant (Taurus)
Zayin (Single)	VI Lovers (Gemini)
Cheth (Single)	VII Temperance (Cancer)
Teth (Single)	VIII Strength (Leo)
Yod (Single)	IX Hermit (Virgo)
Kaph (Double)	X Wheel (Sun)
Lamed (Single)	XI Justice (Libra)
Mem (Mother)	XII Hanged Man (Water)
Nun (Single)	XIII Death (Scorpio)
Samekh (Single)	XIV Chariot (Sagittarius)
Ayin (Single)	XV Devil (Capricorn)
Pe (Double)	XVI Tower (Mars)
Tzaddi (Single)	XVII Star (Aquarius)
Qoph (Single)	XVIII Moon (Pisces)
Resh (Double)	XIX Sun (Jupiter)
Shin (Mother)	XX Judgement (Fire)
Tau (Double)	XXI World (Saturn)

My emendations to the Tarot trump correspondences of the Golden Dawn will not be accepted by everyone who considers them, simply because the system of the Golden Dawn has the inertia of so many years behind it. Numerous books and essays have been written to justify all its aspects, and very good arguments have been called forth in its defense. This modified arrangement of the trumps is offered as my mature and very likely my final statement on the Tarot correspondences. It has evolved slowly over a span of many years, after intense meditations and countless practical applications to test its validity.

If you choose to adopt my correspondences, you can easily make the necessary changes in the ritual structure of Tarot magic to accommodate them. The ordering of the trumps on the circle of the zodiac will be slightly altered from its Golden Dawn sequence, and the planets the Sun and Jupiter will trade places on their planetary modifiers. The trumps of the Mother letters that make up the triangle are unchanged, as are the associations for the individual cards of the Lesser Arcana.

Another departure from the Golden Dawn correspondences that I have used with success for many years involves the location of the four suits on the four directions of the compass. I made this change earlier than my modifications to the trumps, not long after I began the practice of ritual magic. It is described and justified in my first book, *The New Magus*, and in the expanded edition of that work, *New Millennium Magic*. The change is simple enough to describe. In the Golden Dawn correspondences for the Tarot, the suit of Swords and its element Air are linked to the east, and the suit of Pentacles and its element Earth are linked to the north. In my personal system of magic, I invert these locations for the suits. Wands and Fire I leave in the south, and Cups and Water I leave in the west, as they are in the Golden Dawn system.

The north seems to me a natural direction for the airy suit of Swords, because it has always been associated with the cutting winds of winter, at least by those who dwell in the Northern Hemisphere. The east strikes me as suitable for the earthy suit of Pentacles because it is the quarter of spring, and in the springtime new life arises from seeds buried in the ground. Seeds resemble the circular, solid disk that is the emblem of the suit of Pentacles. As for the other two directions, where the suits remain unchanged, the hot south is ideal for fiery Wands, and the west has long been associated in European myth with the mysterious ocean, perhaps because the unexplored Atlantic lay off the eastern coast of the ancient world, making it the best choice for watery Cups.

Golden Dawn	**Tyson**
East: Swords (Air)	*East:* Pentacles (Earth)
South: Wands (Fire)	*South:* Wands (Fire)
West: Cups (Water)	*West:* Cups (Water)
North: Pentacles (Earth)	*North:* Swords (Air)

Why make this inversion of Pentacles and Swords? There are a variety of reasons. One was my desire that it be possible to vibrate the letters of Tetragrammaton in order, when turning a complete circle sunwise around the four directions of space. Under the modified arrangement of the suits, this is possible beginning with the south:

Yod: Wands (Fire), south

Heh: Cups (Water), west

Vau: Swords (Air), north

Heh: Pentacles (Earth), east

My rituals are performed facing the south at the beginning, rather than facing the east, as is the usual Golden Dawn practice. It is the starting point of the circle in my rituals.

Another reason for the shift of the suits in the north and east was my wish that the masculine suits of Swords and Wands be together on the vertical axis of the circle, corresponding with the masculine axis of the Earth, and that the feminine suits of Cups and Pentacles be together on the horizontal axis of the circle, corresponding with the feminine circle of the equator. In my rituals, when I stand facing south or lie within the circle with my feet to the south, this places the masculine Swords and Wands along my body axis at my head and feet, and the feminine Pentacles and Cups on my left and right hands.

The most important justification for the change is that when the heavenly circle of the zodiac is reflected and in this way brought down to the ritual circle on the surface of the ground, the four fixed signs that represent the four elements and the four suits naturally fall as I have allocated them in my modified correspondences. When the reflected zodiac is turned slightly so that Leo (Fire, Wands) occupies the south, Scorpio (Water, Cups) is found in the west, Aquarius (Air, Swords) is found in the north, and Taurus (Earth, Pentacles) is found in the east.

These modifications to the Golden Dawn system have been described here for the benefit of any reader who may wish to experiment with Tarot magic using my own set of correspondences. I would suggest that you only do this after you have completely understood and memorized the Golden Dawn correspondences for the Tarot. It is essential to know the Golden Dawn correspondences perfectly, because they are the standard in modern Western occultism, much more widely used and more highly regarded than any other system. Once you know the Golden Dawn esoteric associations for the Trumps and suit cards, you can if you wish try out my changes to see whether the modifications suit your needs.

GLOSSARY

Altar: In Tarot magic, the altar is composed of the four Aces and resides at the center of the magic circle. It supports the significator of the magician, and provides the central viewpoint for the consciousness of the magician during rituals.

Arcana: The word means "mysteries," and is used for the cards of the Tarot. The Greater Arcana are the twenty-two picture cards, and the Lesser Arcana are the fifty-six suit cards.

Astral: A plane of reality or dimension of consciousness that has form but no substance, similar to the dream world. Magicians project their awareness into the astral world while fully awake for the purpose of manipulating its forms and forces, and to interact with spiritual beings. It is not true that spirits live in the astral world, as is sometimes supposed, but they are most easily perceived by human consciousness on the astral level.

Circle: The circle is made up of the twelve trumps of the Greater Arcana that are related to the twelve signs of the zodiac. They are the Emperor (Aries), the Hierophant (Taurus), the Lovers (Gemini), the Chariot (Cancer), Strength (Leo), the Hermit (Virgo), Justice (Libra), Death (Scorpio), Temperance (Sagittarius), the Devil (Capricorn), the Star (Aquarius), and the Moon (Pisces). The circle provides both a protective barrier, and an enclosed space where magical energy can be accumulated and concentrated.

Court Cards: In each of the four suits there are four cards that bear noble or courtly human figures: the King, Queen, Knight, and Page. These sixteen cards are used in Tarot magic to signify or represent human beings, including the magician who works the ritual. They are for this reason termed significators.

Desire, magic: The magic desire is the motivating intention or urge that drives the achievement of the ritual purpose. It usually has a strong emotional component, and operates for the most part below the level of conscious thought.

Elements: An ancient system that divides the substances of the earthly sphere into four recognized qualities called Fire, Water, Air, and Earth. The elements resemble in their natures and actions the physical substances that give them their names, but they are underlying principles, not the actual substances. Until the age of science, it was believed that everything was composed of a mixture of the four elements. All four elements are located in the sphere of the Earth, but the three more active elements, Fire, Air, and Water, also possess higher or more spiritual aspects that are represented in classical models of the universe as bands or zones just above the Earth, yet below the lowest of the heavenly spheres, that of the Moon. In the Tarot, the four suits represent the four lower tangible elements of the earthly sphere, and the three trumps the Fool, the Hanged Man, and Judgement represent the active, spiritual aspects of Air, Water, and Fire. The element Earth has no higher aspect.

Golden Dawn: The Hermetic Order of the Golden Dawn was a secret Rosicrucian society founded in London in 1888 by three Freemasons for the purpose of studying, teaching, preserving, and practicing ritual magic in the Western tradition.

Grimoire: A word from the French meaning "grammar." Literally, a copybook of practical magic written by a magician as an aid to memory, or as a way of passing on a system of ceremonial magic to a disciple. Grimoires are hand-written texts never intended for public reading, often put together in the form of brief comments or descriptions between prayers and invocations, making them difficult to understand for those who have not studied magic.

Kabbalah: A system of Jewish mysticism that seeks to explain the nature of the universe and humanity's purpose through esoteric interpretations of the Torah. The Kabbalah is divided into a philosophical branch and a practical branch. The practical Kabbalah uses divine names and sacred texts as instruments of magic. The structure known as the Tree of Life, of central importance in the modern Western esoteric tradition, arose from the Kabbalistic doctrine of emanations—ten stages by which the universe was extended from the unknowable essence of God.

Magician: The person who performs magic. Also sometimes called the worker or the ritualist.

Modifiers: The seven trumps associated with the seven planets of traditional astrology. The planetary modifiers are the Magician (Mercury), the High Priestess (Moon), the Empress (Venus), the Wheel (Jupiter), the Tower (Mars), the Sun (Sun), and the World (Saturn). They are called modifiers because they modify the action of the ritual when placed on the zodiacal circle.

Purpose, ritual: The ritual purpose is the reason a ritual is worked. Its fulfillment is expressed symbolically by means of a card, or cards, that are placed upon the triangle of realization.

Realizers: The numbered cards of the four suits from Two to Ten. These cards are called realizers because they realize or actualize the ritual purpose by embodying it in a symbolic way on the triangle of realization.

Ritual: A series of actions designed to achieve a purpose through magic. Effective rituals occur on two levels simultaneously, the physical level and the astral level. The actions of ritual on the astral level often mirror the physical actions of the magician, but it is possible for the physical actions and the astral actions to be different, provided they are symbolically associated or linked. The difference between the physical actions and the astral actions in Tarot magic is more obvious than is usually the case in traditional ceremonial magic.

Sephiroth: (Singular form: Sephirah.) A Hebrew word for the ten stages by which the universe was created. In the simplest sense, it is often assumed to mean the numbers from one to ten. However, the numbers are not the Sephiroth, but are products of the Sephiroth. Each Sephirah, or level of emanation, has occult correspondences such as a divine name, an archangel, a heavenly sphere, and a descriptive title. In the Golden Dawn system, the ten Sephiroth are linked with the ten number cards of the Tarot suits.

Significators: A term that comes from Tarot divination, where the significator is a court card representing the person who seeks the reading. Each of the four suits has four court cards. They are used to represent human beings when working Tarot magic. One significator is selected to stand for the magician. Any other human being who may be directly involved in the ritual is represented by a significator chosen from among the remaining court cards.

Spheres: In the cosmology of the ancient Western world, the Earth is the fixed center of the universe where the four elements interact. Surrounding the Earth are elemental zones of Water, Air, and Fire, representing more spiritual aspects of the three active elements. Above the zones of the active elements are the spheres of the seven wandering bodies of traditional astrology. Above the seven planets is the sphere of the fixed stars, within which is located the band of the zodiac. Above the stars are the divine realms containing the hierarchies of the angels and God. Modern magic continues to make use of this ancient model of the universe.

Symbol: Something that stands for something else. Usually a symbol is a simple thing that represents something more subtle and complex. For example, the symbol of the sword represents the suit of Swords in the Tarot, and the element Air. The symbol of the circle represents a magical barrier that encloses a sacred space.

Tarot: Card decks consisting of seventy-eight cards that are divided into two main parts, the twenty-two trumps or picture cards known as the Greater Arcana, and the fifty-six suit cards known as the Lesser Arcana. The Tarot was invented in Italy during the fifteenth century to play a trick-taking card game of the same name. Its use in magic did not become popular until the nineteenth century, when esoteric Tarot decks began to arise in France.

Tree of Life: A symbolic figure made up of ten circles connected with twenty-two channels. In Golden Dawn magic, the ten circles— which stand for the ten emanations or stages of the process of creation called the Sephiroth—are linked with the number cards of the suits from the Ace to Ten. The twenty-two channels, also known as pathways, are linked with the trumps.

Triangle: In traditional ceremonial magic, the triangle is where spirits are evoked, or called forth into manifest existence. The triangle of realization in Tarot magic is the place where the ritual purpose is realized. It is constructed outside the bounds of the circle from the three elemental trumps the Fool (Air), the Hanged Man (Water), and Judgement (Fire). The point at the apex of the triangle, defined by the Fool, is opened during ritual to create a doorway connecting the desire of the magician within the circle with the realization of that desire within the triangle, and by extension the greater world.

Will: The determination to achieve a purpose, expressing itself as a potent concentration. The will is used during rituals to direct esoteric forms and forces in order to bring about a realization of the magical desire.

WORKS CITED

Budge, E. A. Wallis. *Amulets and Talismans* (originally *Amulets and Superstitions*) [1930]. New York: University Books, 1968.

Cicero, Chic, and Sandra Tabatha Cicero. *The New Golden Dawn Ritual Tarot: Keys to the Rituals, Symbolism, Magic & Divination* [1991]. St. Paul, MN: Llewellyn Publications, 1996.

Crowley, Aleister. *The Book of the Law* [1904]. Quebec: 93 Publishing, 1975.

———. *The Book of Thoth: A Short Essay on the Tarot of the Egyptians* [1944]. New York: Samuel Weiser, 1974.

Decker, Ronald, Thierry Depaulis, and Michael Dummett. *A Wicked Pack of Cards: The Origins of the Occult Tarot*. New York: St. Martin's Press, 1996.

Howe, Ellic. *The Magicians of the Golden Dawn: A Documentary History of a Magical Order 1887–1923* [1972]. New York: Samuel Weiser, 1978.

Kaplan, Stewart R. *The Encyclopedia of Tarot*, vol 1 [1978]. Stamfort, CT: U.S. Games Systems, Inc., 2001.

Leo, Alan. *Esoteric Astrology: A Study in Human Nature*. London: L. N. Fowler & Co. Ltd., 1967.

Regardie, Israel. *The Golden Dawn* [1938–40]. 6th ed. St. Paul, MN: Llewellyn Publications, 1990.

Scholem, Gershom. *Kabbalah* [1974]. Jerusalem: Keter Publishing House, 1977.

Seligmann, Kurt. *The History of Magic.* New York: Pantheon Books, 1948.

Tyson, Donald. *The New Magus.* St. Paul, Minnesota: Llewellyn Publications, 1988.

Westcott, William Wynn, trans. *Sepher Yetzirah: The Book of Formation, with the Fifty Gates of Intelligence and the Thirty-two Paths of Wisdom* [1887]. New York: Samuel Weiser, 1980.

INDEX

Abba, 73
abracadabra, 107–109
Aces, 19, 57, 63, 71–73, 83, 85, 112,
    117–120, 124, 126–127, 139, 147,
    153, 155, 158–159, 167–168, 171,
    177–179, 183, 197–198, 201
Adeptus Minor Ritual, 23–24
agent, 50–51, 88, 153–155, 200
Aima, 74
Aiwass, 36
alchemy, 11, 22
altar, 1–2, 73, 77–78, 83, 85–86,
    88–89, 96, 100, 102, 115–120,
    123–126, 128–129, 153, 155–156,
    158–163, 167–169, 171, 177–183,
    195–198, 201–202, 204
Alverda, Frater Hugo, 23
amulets, 107
Apollo, 10
apport, 52
Arcana, Greater. *See* trumps
aspects, 10, 13, 29, 39, 45, 47, 57, 69,
    71, 131, 135–138, 149–150, 154,
    176, 191, 198, 212
astral, 1, 3–5, 25, 80, 87, 90–91, 96–
    97, 103–104, 113, 116, 119–125,
    127–129, 159–164, 167–171, 178–
    182, 186–187, 192–193, 195, 199,
    201–202, 204–205
astrology, 11, 20, 29–30, 37, 40–43,
    54, 99–100, 125, 131–137, 148,
    151, 154, 157, 160, 177, 190, 207–
    211

Aulam Yesodoth, 71
Babylonians, 99
banishing, 49, 107–108, 140–141,
    167, 170–171
belief, 8, 37, 89, 189
Bembo, Tablet of, 33
Binah, 72–74, 141–144, 174
Book of Formation. See Sepher Yetzirah
Book of Thoth, 36, 39, 57, 59, 175
Book of the Law, 36
Book T, 26, 63
British Museum, 22, 25
Bry, Frater Franciscus de, 23
Budge, E. A. Wallis, 107

candles, 2, 50
Caracalla, 107
Casanova, 11
celestial sphere, 46, 63
Chalices, 18, 47
channels. *See* paths
Chariot, 35, 100, 103, 125, 132–133,
    160, 169, 179, 197, 202, 211–212
Charles VI, 8
charms, 2, 48, 66, 107–109, 185–
    190, 192–194
Chesed, 72–74, 141–143, 145, 174–
    175
Chokmah, 72–74, 141–144, 154
Christian, Paul, 10, 12
Christos, 75, 86
Cicero, Sandra Tabatha, 26

TO WRITE TO THE AUTHOR

If you wish to contact the author or would like more information about this book, please write to the author in care of Llewellyn Worldwide and we will forward your request. Both the author and publisher appreciate hearing from you and learning of your enjoyment of this book and how it has helped you. Llewellyn Worldwide cannot guarantee that every letter written to the author can be answered, but all will be forwarded. Please write to:

Donald Tyson
℅ Llewellyn Worldwide
2143 Wooddale Drive
Woodbury, MN 55125-2989

Please enclose a self-addressed stamped envelope for reply,
or $1.00 to cover costs. If outside U.S.A., enclose
international postal reply coupon.

Many of Llewellyn's authors have websites with additional information and resources. For more information, please visit our website at:

www.llewellyn.com